THE ULTIMATE BIBLE CHARACTER GUIDE

BY GINA DETWILER

THE ULTIMATE BIBLE CHARACTER GUIDE

BY GINA DETWILER

HOLMAN
REFERENCE

Note on name meanings: For some characters, we have included name meanings that are disputed, but we've marked them as uncertain.

Published by B&H Publishing Group, Nashville, Tennessee
BHPublishingGroup.com

Dewey Decimal Classification: C220.92
Subject Heading: BIBLE—BIOGRAPHY / WOMEN IN THE BIBLE / MEN IN THE BIBLE

Printed in China, RRD
2 3 4 5 6 7 • 23 22 21

Written by Gina Detwiler
Managed by Michelle Prater Freeman
Cover design by Faceout Studio, Jeff Miller
Interior design by Faceout Studio, Paul Nielsen

A Boring Bible? Nope.

Anyone who thinks the Bible is boring hasn't read the Bible. It can be many things—enlightening, confusing, mystifying, clarifying, and lifesaving—but it is never boring. It's history from God's perspective. The story of the human race. The story of us. And it's far stranger and more intriguing than you might think.

The Bible is filled not only with captivating stories but also with fascinating people. Writing *The Ultimate Bible Character Guide* has introduced me to many biblical characters I never knew about and shed new light on those I thought I knew so well. Did you know that...

- Enoch and Elijah never died?
- Methuselah lived to be 969 years old?
- Joshua captured thirty-one kings?
- One Canaanite king was assassinated in the bathroom?
- David cut off Goliath's head after killing him?
- The prophet Ezekiel lay on his side in the street for a whole year?
- King Xerxes gave a feast that lasted 180 days?
- John the Baptist ate locusts?
- On the night of His arrest, Jesus' sweat was like drops of blood?

These facts alone are proof that the Bible is the most fascinating book you could ever read. And every word is true.

HOW TO READ THIS BOOK

In *The Ultimate Bible Character Guide*, you will meet bad kings, evil queens, eccentric prophets, giants and giant killers, mysterious priests, lowly criminals, scheming spouses, faithful and unfaithful servants, supernatural beings, flawed heroes, and the flawless Jesus, who came to redeem it all and set in motion the story's end.

The characters are listed in roughly alphabetical order, but you can find out where they fit in history by referring to the biblical timeline on pages 8–27. Contemporaries are also listed to give you an idea of which biblical characters lived at the same time. Refer to the table of contents on pages 6–7 when looking for a specific character.

To discover all these amazing characters, you might choose to read *The Ultimate Bible Character Guide* from front to back. Or you could find your favorite Bible hero and then track all his or her contemporaries, building a better picture of life during that time. Or choose to focus on a particular group of characters . . . kids, kings, bad guys, or supernatural beings. You have more than 150 lives to discover in these pages.

A CHALLENGE

I hope this book fires your imagination and sends you straight to the Bible itself to get "the rest of the story." I also hope it helps you see the people of the Bible as humans like yourself. These are not Marvel heroes and villains; instead they are men, women, and even children who struggled with temptation, fear, and loneliness, who failed often, who lost faith, and who learned many lessons the hard way. Although some chose evil, others trusted God and experienced His grace. And those are the characters who truly triumphed.

So are you ready for a challenge? Find your ultimate characters. Let their stories—their faith and their moments of victory—strengthen you. Let them inspire you to base your life on the Bible with an ultimate goal of living for God and letting Him shape your own amazing story.

CONTENTS

CHARACTERS THROUGH THE AGES

Angels and Demons (ageless)

Michael
P. 160

Gabriel
P. 88

Satan
P. 206

The Age of the Ancients (from before 4000 BC to around 1900 BC)

Adam
Before 4000 BC • P. 36

Cain
Before 4000 BC • P. 60

Enoch
Unknown • P. 79

Eve
Before 4000 BC • P. 84

Abel
Before 4000 BC • P. 30

Abraham
Around 2166 BC • P. 34

Sarah
2100s BC • P. 204

Ham
Unknown • P. 94

Noah
Unknown • P. 176

Lot
In 2100s BC • P. 147

Nimrod
Unknown • P. 175

Melchizedek
Around 2100 BC • P. 159

Hagar
Around 2100 BC • P. 87

The Age of the Ancients (continued)

Job
Before 2000 BC ● P. 124

Ishmael
2000s BC ● P. 101

Leah
1900s BC ● P. 145

Esau
Around 2000 BC ● P. 80

Judah
Around 1920 BCC ● P. 141

Rachel
In 1900s BC ● P. 192

Isaac
2000s BC ● P. 102

Rebekah
Around 2000s BC ● P. 193

Joseph (the dreamer)
Around 1915 BC ● P. 136

Jacob
Around 2000 BC ● P. 106

Benjamin
Around 1900 BC ● P. 55

The Age of Conquest and Judges (from 1500s BC to around 1100 BC)

Aaron
Around 1530 BC ● P. 28

Og
Around 1500 BC ● P. 178

Moses
Around 1526 BC ● P. 164

Caleb
Around 1486 BC ● P. 61

Pharaoh
Around 1500 BC ● P. 184

Joshua
Around 1470s BC ● P. 138

Miriam
1500s BC ● P. 161

Phinehas
Around 1400s BC ● P. 187

The Age of Conquest and Judges (continued)

Eglon
Around 1300 BC • P. 71

Barak
Around 1350 BC • P. 51

Rahab
Around 1430 BC • P. 194

Jael
Around 1300 BC • P. 108

Deborah
Around 1360 BC • P. 68

Jephthah
Around 1250 BC • P. 115

Balaam
Around 1440 BC • P. 49

Gideon
Around 1230 BC • P. 90

Ruth
Around 1175 BC • P. 198

Abimelech
Around 1170 BC • P. 32

Boaz
Around 1200 BC • P. 56

Samson
Around 1100 BC • P. 200

Hannah
Around 1140 BC • P. 96

Naomi
Around 1225 BC • P. 167

Eli
1170 BC • P. 72

Delilah
Around 1100 BC • P. 70

The Age of Royals and Prophets (from around 1100 BC to 400s BC)

Saul
Around 1080 BC ● P. 208

David
Around 1040 BC ● P. 66

Abigail
Around 1030 BC ● P. 31

Goliath
Around 1100 BC ● P. 92

Jonathan
Around 1050 BC ● P. 132

Samuel
Around 1100 BC ● P. 202

Joab
Around 1050 BC ● P. 119

Bathsheba
Around 1010 BC ● P. 53

Solomon
Around 1000 BC • P. 214

Queen of Sheba
Around 1000 BC • P. 191

Asa
Around 932 BC • P. 47

Rehoboam
Around 975 BC • P. 196

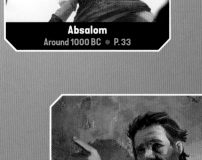

Absalom
Around 1000 BC • P. 33

Jeroboam
Around 950 BC • P. 118

Nathan
Around 1000 BC • P. 168

Ahab
Around 905 BC • P. 38

The Age of Royals and Prophets (continued)

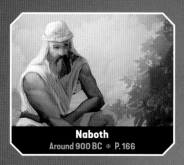

Naboth
Around 900 BC ● P. 166

Elisha
Around 880 BC ● P. 76

Jezebel
Around 900 BC ● P. 122

Jehu
Around 880 BC ● P. 114

Jehoshaphat
Around 900 BC ● P. 113

Athaliah
Around 880 BC ● P. 48

Elijah
Around 900 BC ● P. 74

Jehoram
Around 880 BC ● P. 112

Jonah
In 800s BC ◆ P. 130

Hosea
Around 780 BC ◆ P. 100

Hezekiah
Around 750 BC ◆ P. 97

Amos
Around 780 BC ◆ P. 41

Naaman
850 BCC ◆ P. 163

Ahaz
Around 755 BC ◆ P. 40

Uzziah
Around 800 BC ◆ P. 220

Isaiah
Around 710 BC ◆ P. 104

The Age of Royals and Prophets (continued)

Daniel
Around 621 BC ● P. 64

Manasseh
Around 700 BC ● P. 150

Nebuchadnezzar
Around 630 BC ● P. 170

Zedekiah
Around 620 BC ● P. 224

Josiah
Around 650 BC ● P. 140

Ezekiel
Around 620 BC ● P. 81

Jeremiah
Around 650 BC ● P. 116

Shadrach, Meshach, and Abednego
Around 620 BC ● P. 210

Xerxes
518 BC ● P. 221

Haman
Around 500 BC ● P. 95

Belshazzar
Around 600 BC ● P. 54

Esther
Around 500 BC ● P. 82

Cyrus the Great
Around 599 BC ● P. 63

Nehemiah
Around 500 BC ● P. 172

Mordecai
540 BC ● P. 162

Ezra
Around 480 BC ● P. 86

and Enemies (from around 100 BC to first century AD)

Augustus
63 BC • P. 58

Herod the Great
73 BC • P. 98

Elizabeth
Around 40 BC • P. 73

Zechariah
Around 50 BC • P. 223

Annas
Around 25 BC • P. 45

Anna
Around 100 BC • P. 44

Joseph (Jesus' earthly father)
Around 30 BC • P. 135

Nicodemus
Around 25 BC • P. 174

Joseph of Arimathea
Around 20 BC ◉ P. 134

Peter
Around 10 BC ◉ P. 182

Caiaphas
Around 20 BC ◉ P. 57

Herodias
Around 9 BC ◉ P. 99

Mary
Around 20 BC ◉ P. 152

Pontius Pilate
Around 20 BC ◉ P. 188

Herod Antipas
21 BC ◉ P. 98

John the Baptist
Around 6 BC ● P. 126

Barabbas
Around AD 1 ● P. 50

Jesus Christ
Around 5 BC ● P. 120

John
First century AD ● P. 128

Andrew
Around 5 BC ● P. 43

Jairus
First century AD • P. 109

Judas Iscariot
First century AD • P. 142

Matthew
First century AD • P. 158

James (the brother of Jesus)
First century AD • P. 110

Legion
First century AD • P. 146

Mary and Martha
First century AD • P. 156

James (Son of Thunder)
First century AD • P. 111

Lazarus
First century AD • P. 144

Mark
First century AD • P. 151

Mary Magdalene
First century AD ◆ P. 154

Stephen
First century AD ◆ P. 216

Philip (a brainy apostle)
First century AD ◆ P. 186

Samaritan Woman
First century AD ◆ P. 197

Thomas
First century AD ◆ P. 217

Nathanael
First century AD ◆ P. 169

Zacchaeus
First century AD ◆ P. 222

The Age of the Early Christians and Their Challengers (from around 4 BC to first century AD)

Herod Agrippa I
Around 10 BC • P. 99

Herod Agrippa II
27 AD • P. 99

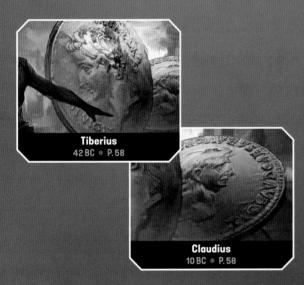

Tiberius
42 BC • P. 58

Claudius
10 BC • P. 58

Nero
37 AD • P. 58

Paul
Around 4 BC • P. 180

The Age of the Early Christians and Their Challengers (continued)

Barnabas
First century AD ⊕ P. 52

Cornelius
First century AD ⊕ P. 62

Ananias and Sapphira
First century AD ⊕ P. 42

Elymas
First century AD ⊕ P. 78

Apollos
First century AD ⊕ P. 46

Luke
First century AD ⊕ P. 148

Priscilla and Aquila
First century AD ◈ P. 190

Timothy
First century AD ◈ P. 218

Lydia
First century AD ◈ P. 149

Silas
First century AD ◈ P. 212

Titus
First century AD ◈ P. 219

Philip (the evangelist)
First century AD ◈ P. 179

Simon Magus
First century AD ◈ P. 213

AARON

MOSES' BIG BROTHER

STORY IN BIBLE Exodus, Leviticus, Numbers, Deuteronomy

BORN Around 1530 BC in Egypt

NAME MEANING "Mountain of Strength" (uncertain)

OCCUPATION High priest

RELATIVES Father—Amram. Mother—Jochebed. Sister—Miriam. Brother—Moses. Wife—Elisheba. Sons—Nadab, Abihu, Eleazar, Ithamar.

CLAIM TO FAME Israel's first high priest

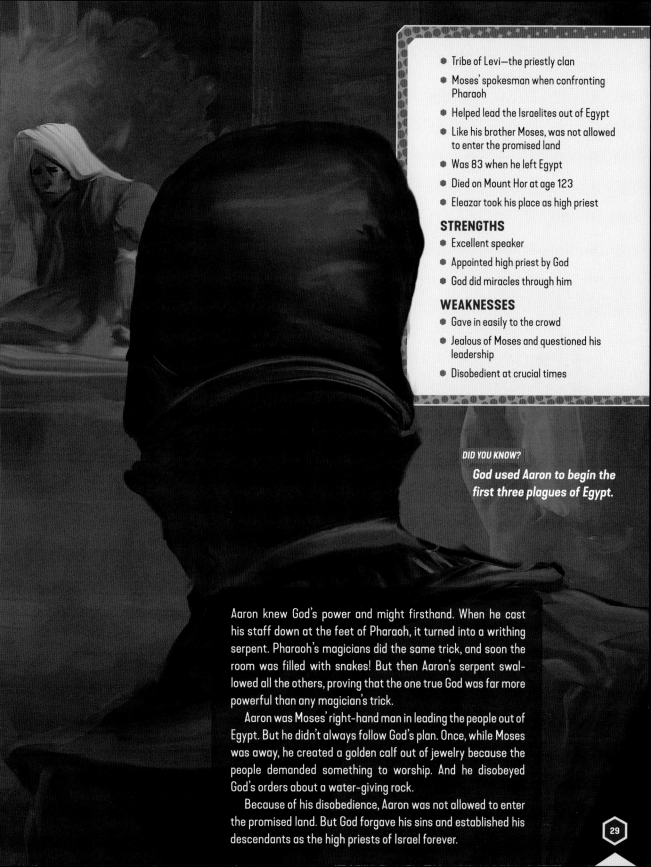

- Tribe of Levi—the priestly clan
- Moses' spokesman when confronting Pharaoh
- Helped lead the Israelites out of Egypt
- Like his brother Moses, was not allowed to enter the promised land
- Was 83 when he left Egypt
- Died on Mount Hor at age 123
- Eleazar took his place as high priest

STRENGTHS

- Excellent speaker
- Appointed high priest by God
- God did miracles through him

WEAKNESSES

- Gave in easily to the crowd
- Jealous of Moses and questioned his leadership
- Disobedient at crucial times

DID YOU KNOW?

God used Aaron to begin the first three plagues of Egypt.

Aaron knew God's power and might firsthand. When he cast his staff down at the feet of Pharaoh, it turned into a writhing serpent. Pharaoh's magicians did the same trick, and soon the room was filled with snakes! But then Aaron's serpent swallowed all the others, proving that the one true God was far more powerful than any magician's trick.

Aaron was Moses' right-hand man in leading the people out of Egypt. But he didn't always follow God's plan. Once, while Moses was away, he created a golden calf out of jewelry because the people demanded something to worship. And he disobeyed God's orders about a water-giving rock.

Because of his disobedience, Aaron was not allowed to enter the promised land. But God forgave his sins and established his descendants as the high priests of Israel forever.

ABEL

THE WORLD'S FIRST MURDER VICTIM

STORY IN BIBLE Genesis 4

BORN Before 4000 BC

NAME MEANING "Breath"

OCCUPATION Shepherd

RELATIVES Father—Adam. Mother—Eve. Brother—Cain, Seth.

CLAIM TO FAME Murdered by his brother Cain

- Second son of Adam and Eve
- Had strong faith in God
- Gave God a pleasing offering of a firstborn lamb
- Killed in a field by his brother Cain, whose offer was not accepted by God
- His blood cried out for vengeance to God

STORY IN BIBLE 1 Samuel 25, 1 Chronicles 3

BORN Around 1030 BC

OCCUPATION Wife

NAME MEANING "My Father Rejoices"

RELATIVES First husband—Nabal. Second husband—David. Son—Chileab (Daniel).

CLAIM TO FAME Stopped a revengeful attack by making dinner

Abigail was the wife of a wealthy and wicked sheep owner named Nabal. One day David and his warriors came to Nabal's farm asking for food in exchange for protecting Nabal's properties. Nabal not only refused, but he also insulted David so badly that David decided to attack him. But Abigail was not only beautiful, she was also smart. She prepared a huge feast, loaded it on donkeys, and took it to David. It was the Bible's first take-out dinner. She apologized for the bad behavior of her husband, whose name means "stupid." When Nabal learned what his wife had done, he got so upset he "became a stone" and died after ten days. David asked Abigail to be his wife, and she said yes. When she was kidnapped by raiders a few years later, David went after them and brought her back safely.

ABIMELECH | *BAD BROTHER*

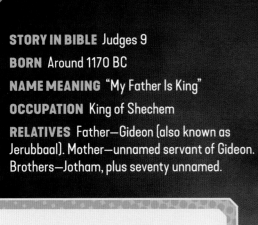

STORY IN BIBLE Judges 9

BORN Around 1170 BC

NAME MEANING "My Father Is King"

OCCUPATION King of Shechem

RELATIVES Father—Gideon (also known as Jerubbaal). Mother—unnamed servant of Gideon. Brothers—Jotham, plus seventy unnamed.

- He was the greedy, conniving son of the hero Gideon
- He conspired with his mother's family in Shechem to murder all seventy of his half-brothers so he could be named king. Only one brother, Jotham, escaped.
- The leaders of Shechem made Abimelech king.
- Jotham laid a curse on all the men who had helped make Abimelech king.
- He ruled for three years.
- God sent an evil spirit between Abimelech and the city leaders.
- People rebelled against Abimelech.
- Abimelech brutally crushed the rebellion, killing everyone and razing the villages to the ground.
- As he was attacking a tall tower, a woman threw a millstone down onto his head and crushed his skull.
- Abimelech told his armor-bearer to kill him so it wouldn't be said he was killed by a woman.

ABSALOM

- Third son of David
- Handsome, with long, thick, flowing hair
- Fine warrior
- Declared himself king and started a revolt against his father
- Forced David into exile
- Lost the battle when David returned to challenge him
- Tried to flee on a mule, but his hair got tangled in a tree branch
- Killed by David's general Joab (against David's orders) as he hung from the tree by his hair

STORY IN BIBLE
2 Samuel 13–18

BORN Around 1000 BC in Hebron

NAME MEANING "Father Is Peace"

OCCUPATION Warrior

RELATIVES Father—David. Mother—Maacah. Siblings—Amnon, Tamar, and many others.

CLAIM TO FAME Led a rebellion against his father, King David

33

ABRAHAM | *GOD'S BEST FRIEND*

STORY IN BIBLE Genesis 11–25

BORN Around 2166 BC

NAME MEANING "Father of the Multitude"

OCCUPATION Rancher, part-time warrior

RELATIVES Father—Terah. Wife—Sarah. Brothers—Nahor and Haran. Nephew— Lot. Sons—Ishmael, Isaac, and six more.

CLAIM TO FAME Founder of the Jewish nation

God told Abraham he would be the father of a great nation. But as Abraham got older and older, no child was born to him. Then one day, when Abraham was ninety-nine years old, three men came to visit him. One of the men told him that within a year, Abraham would have a son. Turns out the men weren't really humans at all, but the Lord Himself and two angels.

Still, Abraham had trouble believing them. His wife Sarah was eighty-nine years old, too old to have a child. But Abraham trusted the Lord, despite his doubts. And sure enough, a year later, Sarah gave birth to a baby boy named Isaac. Abraham was overjoyed.

A few years later, God told Abraham to take his only son Isaac up a mountain and sacrifice him. Abraham must have been extremely confused and fearful, but again he trusted the Lord and obeyed His instructions. He took Isaac up to Mount Moriah, where he prepared an altar and placed his beloved son on it. But just as Abraham raised the knife to sacrifice his son, the angel of the Lord called out to stop him. The Lord had tested Abraham and found him faithful. From then on, the Lord blessed Abraham and promised to make his descendants as numerous as the stars in the sky.

- Original name was Abram, "exalted father"
- Born to a pagan family in Ur (in modern-day Iraq)
- Told by God to leave his family and move to a new land
- God changed his name to Abraham and made a covenant with him to make him into a great nation.
- Wandered for decades
- Exiled to Egypt for a time
- Rescued his nephew Lot when he was captured during war
- Blessed by Melchizedek, the mysterious priest
- Tried to save Sodom from being destroyed by God
- God called Abraham His friend.

STRENGTHS
- Known for his faith and obedience to God
- Courageous in the face of danger
- Wealthy, generous, and honorable

WEAKNESSES
- Sometimes didn't tell the truth
- Didn't always follow directions well

DID YOU KNOW?
Abraham is mentioned 307 times in twenty-seven books of the Bible.

ADAM
FIRST MAN ON EARTH

STORY IN BIBLE Genesis 1–3

BORN Fully grown in garden of Eden, before 4000 BC

NAME MEANING "Mankind"

OCCUPATION Gardener and zoologist

FAMILY Wife—Eve. Children—Cain, Abel, Seth, and many more.

CLAIM TO FAME First human

DID YOU KNOW?
We don't know what kind of fruit the "forbidden fruit" was.

- Lived in the garden of Eden
- Named the animals and tended the garden
- Lived to be 930

STRENGTHS
- Had a personal relationship with God
- Had a perfect life for a while

WEAKNESSES
- Blamed others rather than taking responsibility for his actions
- Tried to hide his sin from God

Adam was the world's first human. He was never a baby or a kid. After five days of making the whole world and everything in it, God created Adam out of dirt and breathed His own breath into his nostrils, bringing this new man to life. Only God could make a human out of dirt.

Then God created a woman to be Adam's wife and partner. She was called Eve.

Adam had a very close relationship with God. In fact, God would often come down to the garden and take walks with Adam in the evenings. The garden was like an intersection between heaven and earth. The best of both worlds. Adam had it made.

Things were going well until Eve gave him some fruit to eat from the one tree in the garden that God had told them never to eat from: the Tree of the Knowledge of Good and Evil. Because of their sin, God placed some pretty tough curses on each of them. Then He banished them from the garden. To keep them out, He blocked the path with a "flaming, whirling sword." Adam became the world's first farmer. Then Adam became the world's first father. But that's another story.

Although Adam's life was now hard, all was not lost, for one day God would redeem the human race through His own Son, Jesus, who is also called the "Second Adam."

AHAB
THE KING WITH TWO GODS

STORY IN BIBLE 1 Kings 16–18, 20–22

BORN Around 905 BC in Judah

NAME MEANING "Father's Brother"

OCCUPATION Seventh king of Israel (northern kingdom)

RELATIVES Father—Omri. Wife—Jezebel. Daughter—Athaliah. Sons—Ahaziah, Jehoram.

CONTEMPORARIES Elijah, Micaiah, Ben-hadad (king of Syria), Jehoshaphat (king of Judah)

CLAIM TO FAME Led Israel into idolatry

DID YOU KNOW?

Captain Ahab, a character in the novel Moby-Dick, has many similarities to King Ahab.

- Married the wicked pagan princess Jezebel against God's law and let her kill God's prophets
- His sin caused a three-year drought in Israel, which ended when Elijah challenged the priests of Baal to a showdown
- Had his neighbor Naboth murdered to get his vineyard
- Briefly repented when Elijah told him dogs would lick up his blood

STRENGTHS
- Mighty military leader
- Relatively peaceful reign
- Built beautiful cities

WEAKNESSES
- Unduly influenced by his pagan wife
- Worshiped idols
- Disobeyed God's commands
- Committed murder

Ahab might have been a great king had he not been influenced by Jezebel. Even while worshiping Baal and Asherah, he continued to worship God. The prophet Elijah told him and his people that they had to choose: "How long will you waver between two opinions? If the LORD is God, follow him. But if Baal, follow him."

Ahab never made that choice. Before going to war with Syria, the prophet Micaiah told him he would lose the battle and die. The prophet then reported that God had sent a "lying spirit" to entice Ahab into war. The "lying spirit" came in the form of four hundred false prophets who told Ahab he would win.

Ahab was angry about the prophecy and had Micaiah thrown in prison. Still, he tried to protect himself by going into battle dressed as an ordinary soldier, without his royal robes. It didn't work. A stray arrow hit him between the joints of his armor. He remained propped up in his chariot as he slowly bled to death, watching as the battle was lost. After his death, his chariot was washed of the blood in the pool of Samaria, and dogs came to lick it up, just as Elijah had prophesied.

AHAZ
A MOST EVIL KING

STORY IN BIBLE 2 Kings 16, 2 Chronicles 28, Isaiah 7

BORN Around 755 BC in Judah

NAME MEANING "He (God) Has Grasped"

OCCUPATION Eleventh king of Judah

RELATIVES Father—Jotham. Son—Hezekiah.

CONTEMPORARIES Pekah (king of Israel), Tiglath-pileser III (king of Assyria), Isaiah

CLAIM TO FAME Led Judah into idolatry

- Took throne at age twenty
- Reigned for sixteen miserable years
- Sacrificed his own children to the pagan bull-god Moloch
- Remodeled the temple to look like a pagan temple
- Refused to heed Isaiah's warning to worship the Lord alone
- Was attacked by Israel, Edom, Philistia, and Assyria at the Lord's direction
- Over 100,000 of his people were killed, and 200,000 were carried off to captivity
- Stole the valuable items from the temple and gave them to the king of Assyria to buy protection (it didn't work)
- His people refused to bury him in the royal tomb
- Listed in the genealogy of Jesus

THE SHEPHERD PROPHET

AMOS

STORY IN BIBLE Book of Amos

BORN Around 780 BC

NAME MEANING "Burden Bearer"

OCCUPATION Sheep breeder and prophet

CONTEMPORARIES Uzziah (king of Judah). Jeroboam II (king of Israel)

CLAIM TO FAME Warned of bad times to come

- Not formally educated like other prophets
- From Judah but was sent to Israel (northern kingdom) to preach
- Owned a fig orchard and raised sheep
- Despite the prosperity of the kingdom, prophesied bad news
- Known for blunt and fiery speeches
- Told the people to start worshiping only God and stop oppressing the poor or else
- Charged with treason and kicked out of Israel
- Prophecies fulfilled when Israel was conquered only a generation later

ANANIAS AND SAPPHIRA

WOLVES IN SHEEP'S CLOTHING

STORY IN BIBLE Acts 5

BORN First century AD

NAME MEANING Ananias—"The Lord Has Dealt Graciously." Sapphira—"Beautiful."

OCCUPATION Landowners

CONTEMPORARIES Peter, Barnabas

CLAIM TO FAME Tried to deceive God and paid the price

Ananias and Sapphira were eager to be a part of the early church in Jerusalem. They saw that other believers had been greatly praised for selling land and giving the proceeds to the church. So they sold some land but only gave a portion of the money to the church. Their desire was not to help the church, but to gain favor and get lots of praise for their actions.

When asked if they had given all the money from the land sale, Ananias lied and said yes. Peter saw his heart nd asked, "why has Satan filled your heart to lie to the Holy Spirit?" Ananias dropped dead on the spot! His wife Sapphira came in three hours later, repeated the same lie, and died beside her husband. Ananias and Sapphira quickly became examples of how lying and hypocrisy were not ways to show one's devotion to God.

STORY IN BIBLE Matthew, Mark, Luke, John, Acts 1

BORN Around 5 BC in Bethsaida

NAME MEANING "Manly" (uncertain)

OCCUPATION Fisherman

RELATIVES Father—Jonas. Brother—Simon Peter.

CONTEMPORARIES John the Baptist, Jesus, the disciples

CLAIM TO FAME Introduced Peter to Jesus

- Fisherman on Sea of Galilee
- Lived in Capernaum with brother and mother-in-law
- Brother of Simon Peter
- Originally a disciple of John the Baptist
- First disciple of Jesus
- Told Peter he had "found the Messiah" and introduced him to Jesus
- Quieter, more reserved than Peter
- Found the boy with the five loaves and two fish before the feeding of the 5,000
- Questioned Jesus about the coming destruction of the temple and end times events
- Possibly preached in Greece after Jesus' resurrection
- Believed to have been martyred on an X-shaped cross

ANNA   OLD FAITHFUL

STORY IN BIBLE Luke 2

BORN Around 100 BC

NAME MEANING "Gracious"

OCCUPATION Prophetess

RELATIVES Father—Phanuel

CONTEMPORARIES Mary, Joseph, Simeon

CLAIM TO FAME Proclaimed Jesus the Messiah

- Prophetess in the temple of Jerusalem
- From the tribe of Asher
- Probably over 100 years old
- Had been a widow for 84 years
- Spent all her days fasting and praying in the temple, awaiting the arrival of the Messiah
- When she saw the infant Jesus, she thanked and praised God for fulfilling the promise He had made
- Spoke about Jesus to all who looked forward to the "redemption of Jerusalem"

ANNAS

STORY IN BIBLE | John 18; Acts 4
BORN | Around 25 BC
NAME MEANING | "Merciful"
OCCUPATION | High priest
RELATIVES | Father—Seth. Son-in-Law—Caiaphas.
CLAIM TO FAME | Participated in Jesus' trial

- Former high priest and father-in-law of the current high priest, Caiaphas

- First to question Jesus after His arrest

- Greedy and corrupt

- Member of the Sanhedrin, the Jewish court

- Hated Jesus, possibly because his family made a lot of money from selling animal sacrifices in the temple, which Jesus condemned

- Sat in judgment of Peter and John when they were arrested for preaching about Jesus and healing people

APOLLOS BOLD SPEAKER

STORY IN BIBLE Acts 18; 1 Corinthians 3

BORN First century AD

NAME MEANING "Destroyer" (uncertain)

OCCUPATION Preacher in Ephesus and Corinth

CONTEMPORARIES Paul, Priscilla, Aquila

CLAIM TO FAME Preached about Jesus to the Gentiles (non-Jews)

- Christian Jew from Alexandria, Egypt
- Called by God to preach about Jesus in Ephesus and Corinth
- A powerful, eloquent preacher
- Knew the teaching of John the Baptist but not the whole story of Jesus' mission
- Helped establish the church in Corinth

- Was schooled in the whole gospel by Priscilla and Aquila, friends of Paul
- Was dismayed when the church split into two factions—those following Apollos and those following Paul.
- Paul encouraged the Corinthians in a letter not to follow either him or Apollos, only Jesus Christ

STORY IN BIBLE 1 Kings 15; 2 Chronicles 14—16

BORN Around 932 BC

NAME MEANING "Healer"

OCCUPATION Third king of Judah, 913—873 BC

RELATIVES Grandmother—Maacah. Father—Abijam, also spelled Abijah. Grandfather—Rehoboam. Son—Jehoshaphat.

CONTEMPORARIES Ben-hadad (king of Aram), Baasha (king of Israel)

CLAIM TO FAME Restored Judah to worship one true God

- Reigned for 41 years
- Humble king who became prideful later in life
- Got rid of the idols and pagan altars
- Restored proper worship of the Lord in the temple
- Removed his grandmother from the throne because she worshiped idols
- Reigned during a long period of prosperity and peace
- When threatened by King Baasha of Israel, made an unwise alliance with the Assyrian king, offering him riches from the temple
- Had the prophet Hanani thrown in prison when he rebuked the king for his actions
- When struck with a terrible foot disease, Asa did not turn back to God, putting all his faith in the physicians. They couldn't cure him, and he died.

ATHALIAH | LIKE MOTHER, LIKE DAUGHTER

2 Kings 11; 2 Chronicles 21–23

Around 880 BC

"The Lord Has Announced His Exalted Nature"

Queen of Judah

Husband—Jehoram (king of Judah). Father—Ahab (king of Israel). Mother—Jezebel. Son—Ahaziah. Grandson—Joash. Sister-in-law—Jehoshabeath.

Elijah, Jehu, Jehoiada (priest)

The only ruling queen in the history of Judah

When Princess Athaliah of Israel married Prince Jehoram of Judah, in an alliance formed between the two kingdoms, she set out to do in Judah what her mother Jezebel had done in Israel: turn her husband and all the people from worshiping the Lord to worshiping idols. She was very successful. But when her husband died from a terrible intestinal disease (inflicted by the Lord for his many sins), and her son was assassinated, Athaliah decided she wanted to rule Judah in her own name. So she quickly had all of her own grandsons—Jehoram's legal heirs—murdered.

Athaliah reigned for six years. Little did she know that her youngest grandson, Joash, still lived, saved by Jehoram's daughter Jehosheba and hidden in a bedroom by her husband, the priest Jehoiada. After six years, Jehoiada staged a coup. He revealed Joash to the people and had him crowned the rightful king in the temple. When Athaliah heard about it, she tore her clothes in rage. But she didn't rage for long, because Jehoiada had her taken away and executed.

STORY IN BIBLE Numbers 22–24

BORN Around 1440 BC

NAME MEANING "Devourer of a Nation"

OCCUPATION Sorcerer and prophet

RELATIVES Father—Beor

CONTEMPORARIES Balak (king of Moab), Moses

CLAIM TO FAME Hired to curse Israel but blessed her instead

Balaam wasn't a Jew, but he believed in the Lord. He was a prophet who had grown rich from handing out curses and blessings. When the Moabite King Balak asked him to come to his kingdom to curse the Israelites, Balaam asked for God's permission. After initially refusing, God allowed Balaam to go on the journey as long as he said what the Lord wanted him to say.

But while on the road, Balaam may have had a change of heart about following the Lord's instructions. For suddenly his donkey pulled over to the side of the road and refused to budge. Balaam whipped the donkey until it turned to him and started speaking. Balaam was astounded that his donkey was talking to him. But then he looked up and saw what the donkey had seen: a huge angel blocking his path. The angel rebuked Balaam and reminded him to say only what the Lord wanted him to say. When Balaam got to Moab, instead of cursing the Israelites, he blessed them. King Balak was so angry he sent Balaam home without paying him a penny.

BARABBAS
ONE LUCKY CRIMINAL

STORY IN BIBLE Matthew 27; Mark 15;
Luke 23; John 18

BORN Around AD 1

NAME MEANING "Son of Father"

OCCUPATION Criminal

CLAIM TO FAME Was pardoned instead of Jesus

- Notorious murderer and rebel
- Extremely violent
- Sentenced to die at the time of Jesus' arrest
- Pontius Pilate offered a prisoner to be released in celebration of the Passover, hoping the crowd would pick Jesus.
- The crowd chose Barabbas to be freed.
- After his release, Barabbas disappeared from history.

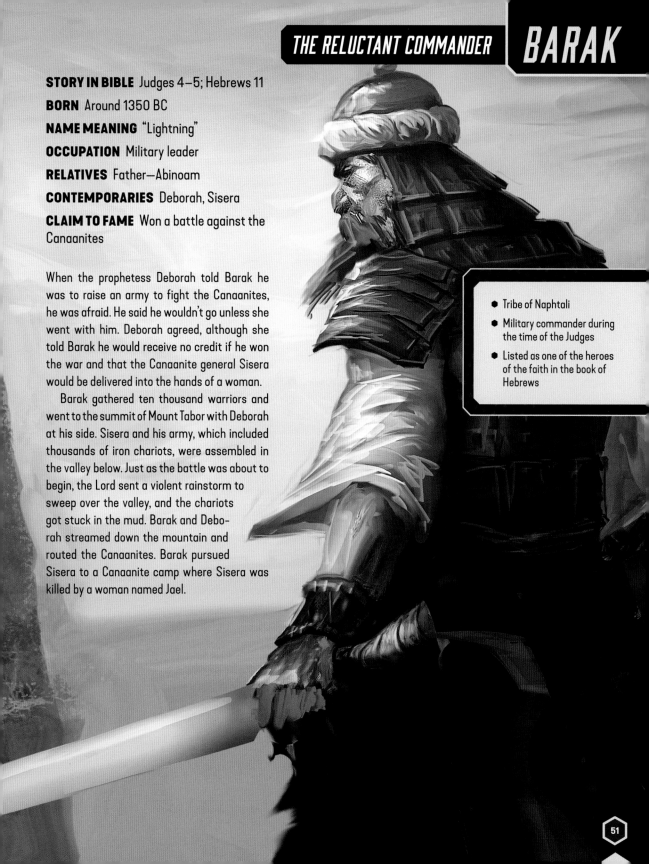

THE RELUCTANT COMMANDER | BARAK

STORY IN BIBLE Judges 4–5; Hebrews 11

BORN Around 1350 BC

NAME MEANING "Lightning"

OCCUPATION Military leader

RELATIVES Father—Abinoam

CONTEMPORARIES Deborah, Sisera

CLAIM TO FAME Won a battle against the Canaanites

When the prophetess Deborah told Barak he was to raise an army to fight the Canaanites, he was afraid. He said he wouldn't go unless she went with him. Deborah agreed, although she told Barak he would receive no credit if he won the war and that the Canaanite general Sisera would be delivered into the hands of a woman.

Barak gathered ten thousand warriors and went to the summit of Mount Tabor with Deborah at his side. Sisera and his army, which included thousands of iron chariots, were assembled in the valley below. Just as the battle was about to begin, the Lord sent a violent rainstorm to sweep over the valley, and the chariots got stuck in the mud. Barak and Deborah streamed down the mountain and routed the Canaanites. Barak pursued Sisera to a Canaanite camp where Sisera was killed by a woman named Jael.

- Tribe of Naphtali
- Military commander during the time of the Judges
- Listed as one of the heroes of the faith in the book of Hebrews

BARNABAS

THE ENCOURAGER

- Jewish man from Cyprus (a Greek island)
- Originally called Joseph
- Sold his property and moved to Jerusalem to join the Christian movement
- Called an apostle, although not one of the original twelve
- Known for his encouragement of the followers of Jesus
- Introduced Paul to the apostles after his conversion
- Due to his intervention, the apostles accepted Paul, who had been a persecutor of the early church
- Traveled with Paul on several missionary journeys
- Dubbed "Zeus" by the people of Lystra for his commanding presence
- Helped Paul establish a church in Antioch
- Brought relief funds to Jerusalem during a famine
- Parted ways with Paul over a disagreement concerning his cousin Mark

STORY IN BIBLE Acts 4; 9; 11; 13; 14

BORN First century AD

NAME MEANING "Son of Encouragement"

OCCUPATION Apostle

RELATIVES Cousin—Mark

CONTEMPORARIES Paul, the apostles

CLAIM TO FAME Preached alongside Paul to the Gentiles (non-Jews)

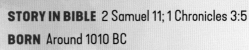

STORY IN BIBLE 2 Samuel 11; 1 Chronicles 3:5

BORN Around 1010 BC

NAME MEANING "Daughter of Abundance"

OCCUPATION Wife and mother

RELATIVES Father—Eliam. First Husband—Uriah. Second husband—David. Sons—Solomon, Shimea, Shobab, Nathan.

CLAIM TO FAME The object of King David's great sin

- She was the very beautiful wife of Uriah the Hethite, one of David's top fighters (Hethites were Gentiles).

- David saw her and wanted her to be his wife.

- David had Uriah killed so he could marry Bathsheba.

- She became David's seventh wife.

- Because of David's sin, her first son died.

- Her second child, Solomon, would become David's heir and the next king of Israel.

- She bore three more children.

- She prevented a plot by David's son Adonijah to take the throne from Solomon.

BELSHAZZAR | *THE LAST PARTIER IN BABYLON*

STORY IN BIBLE Daniel 5

BORN Around 600 BC in Babylon

NAME MEANING "Bel's Prince"

OCCUPATION Co-regent of Babylon

RELATIVES Father—Nabonidus

CONTEMPORARIES Daniel, Cyrus

CLAIM TO FAME Saw the writing on the wall

- Acted as king while his father, Nabonidus, the actual king, was out campaigning in Arabia

- Kind of a party animal

- Gave a lavish party for the leaders of Babylon

- Ordered his servants to bring the gold and silver cups stolen from the temple in Jerusalem for his guests to drink from

- Collapsed in fright when a giant hand appeared and wrote on the wall: MENE, MENE, TEKEL, and PARSIN

- Only Daniel could explain the message, which meant, "Your days are numbered. You've been weighed and found wanting. Your kingdom has been given to the Medes and Persians."

- Killed that very night when the city was invaded by the Persian army, which had diverted the waters of the Euphrates River to dry out the moat protecting the city

BENJAMIN

STORY IN BIBLE Genesis 35–40

BORN Around 1900 BC

NAME MEANING "My Right-Hand Son"

OCCUPATION Shepherd, herdsman

RELATIVES Father—Jacob. Mother—Rachel. Brothers—Joseph and ten more.

CLAIM TO FAME Beloved of Jacob and Joseph

- Youngest son of Jacob
- Full brother of Joseph, whom the brothers sold into slavery
- Born on the road from Bethel to Bethlehem
- Named "Ben-oni" by his dying mother at his birth, which means "son of my sorrow"
- Name changed to Benjamin by Jacob
- Favored by Jacob after Joseph disappeared
- Jacob prophesied that his descendants would be great warriors

Benjamin stayed home with his father when his brothers went to Egypt to beg for food during a famine. Little did they know that their brother Joseph was now second in command in Egypt. Joseph demanded the brothers fetch Benjamin from his father's house. When they complied, Joseph planted a golden cup in Benjamin's sack and pretended Benjamin had stolen it. But Judah stepped up to take the blame. Joseph was so moved that he revealed his true identity, and the brothers had a wonderful reunion.

BOAZ | *THE KINSMAN REDEEMER*

STORY IN BIBLE Book of Ruth; Matthew 1:5

BORN Around 1200 BC

NAME MEANING "Lively"

OCCUPATION Farmer

RELATIVES Father—Salmon. Wife—Ruth.

CLAIM TO FAME Married the widow Ruth and restored her family

- Wealthy landowner in Bethlehem
- A descendant of Rahab, the Canaanite woman who hid the Israelite spies before the destruction of Jericho
- Extremely kind, generous, modeled God's heart for His people
- Helped Ruth and her mother-in-law, Naomi, by buying back the land of his relative for them
- Fell in love with Ruth, a Moabite widow and the daughter-in-law of his dead relative Elimelech, when he saw her picking up grain from his fields
- Married Ruth, even though she was not a Jew
- Listed in the genealogy of Jesus

STORY IN BIBLE Matthew 26; John 11

BORN Around 20 BC

NAME MEANING "Depression"

OCCUPATION High priest

RELATIVES Father-in-law—Annas

CONTEMPORARIES Pontius Pilate, Jesus

CLAIM TO FAME Orchestrated the execution of Jesus

- Head of the Sanhedrin, the high court
- Other than Pilate, the most powerful man in Judea
- Wanted Jesus put to death after learning He had raised Lazarus from the dead
- Worried that Jesus' activities would cause an uprising, forcing the Romans to intervene
- Presided over Jesus' illegal trial
- Tore his robes when Jesus admitted to being the Christ
- Charged Jesus with blasphemy
- Presided over the trial of Peter and John after Christ's resurrection
- Unwittingly proclaimed Jesus' whole mission when he said, "You know nothing at all! You're not considering that it is to your advantage that one man should die for the people rather than the whole nation perish" (John 11:49–50).

THE CAESARS

ROMAN RULERS DURING THE TIME OF JESUS AND THE EARLY CHURCH

AUGUSTUS
(reigned 27 BC–AD 14)

- Adopted son of Julius Caesar
- Ruthless dictator
- Defeated Antony and Cleopatra in Egypt
- Claimed to be a god
- Ordered a census of Judea so that every man had to return to his own home-town, which is why Joseph and Mary went to Bethlehem where Jesus was born

TIBERIUS (reigned AD 14–37)

- Ruled during the public ministry of Jesus
- Stepson of Augustus
- Very successful military leader
- Gave Jews the freedom to observe their own laws and customs in their homelands
- Herod Antipas named a city after him
- Appointed Pontius Pilate as governor of Judea
- Had many of Rome's leaders falsely accused of crimes and executed
- Because his own sons died, he was succeeded by his great-nephew Caligula, who turned out to be quite insane.

CLAUDIUS (reigned AD 41–54)

- Tiberius's nephew, took over from Caligula
- Somewhat deaf and walked with a limp
- Gave Jews freedom of worship in their own lands
- Friends with Herod Agrippa, who helped secure his throne
- Gave Herod Agrippa full control of Judea
  - Expelled Christian Jews from Rome, including Priscilla and Aquila
    - Several famines occurred during his reign
      - Murdered by his wife
        - Proclaimed a god by the Roman senate

NERO (reigned AD 54–68)

- Stepson of Claudius
- The last caesar to rule as emperor
- Had his mother, brother, and wife murdered
- Considered himself a god
- Spent most of his time on his personal pleasures
- Blamed Christians when Rome burned in AD 64
- Persecuted Christians, often having them thrown into the arena to be killed by lions
- Both Peter and Paul were executed under Nero's reign
- The Jewish revolt against his persecutions led Rome to invade Judea and destroy Jerusalem a few years later
- Committed suicide

CAIN | *WORLD'S FIRST MURDERER*

STORY IN BIBLE Genesis 4

BORN Before 4000 BC

NAME MEANING "Metalworker" (uncertain)

OCCUPATION Farmer

RELATIVES Father—Adam. Mother—Eve. Brothers—Abel, Seth. Son—Enoch.

CLAIM TO FAME Killed his brother out of jealousy

- Firstborn of Adam and Eve
- Raised crops and worked the land
- Had his offering of crops rejected by the Lord
- Jealous that brother Abel's offering was accepted
- Lured Abel out to the field and murdered him
- The Lord cursed the ground Cain farmed so nothing would grow
- Became a fugitive and a wanderer, fearing the Lord would kill him too
- The Lord had mercy on Cain and put a mark on him, protecting him from anyone who would try to attack him.
- Settled in a land called Nod, east of Eden
- Built a city in Nod and named it after his son, Enoch
- Had a large family of craftsmen, musicians, and herdsmen

STORY IN BIBLE Numbers 13–14; Joshua 14–15

BORN Around 1486 BC

NAME MEANING "Rages Like a Dog"

OCCUPATION Warrior

RELATIVES Father—Jephunneh. Brother—Kenaz.

CONTEMPORARIES Joshua, Moses

SIGNIFICANCE Helped lead the conquest of the promised land

- Lived during the time of the exodus
- Trusted God
- Great warrior
- A Kenizzite, a tribe descended from Esau and absorbed into the tribe of Judah
- One of only two people who left Egypt and entered the promised land

Before the Israelites entered the promised land, Caleb was one of twelve spies sent by Moses to scout the land and bring back a report. The men returned with terrifying tales of giants living in huge, fortified cities. Caleb and Joshua advised the Israelites to take the land, knowing God had given it to them. But the others refused. For their disobedience, the other ten men were struck with a plague and died, and the Israelites had to spend another forty years in the wilderness.

Caleb and Joshua did invade Canaan forty-five years later. At the age of eighty-five, Caleb went up to the hill country of Hebron and killed or drove out the race of giants known as the Anakim. The Lord gave him the territory of Hebron as his inheritance because of his unwavering loyalty.

CORNELIUS
FIRST CHRISTIAN SOLDIER

STORY IN BIBLE Acts 10–11

BORN First century AD

NAME MEANING "Horn" (uncertain)

OCCUPATION Roman centurion

RELATIVES Wife—Unnamed. Children—Unnamed.

CONTEMPORARIES Peter, Philip

CLAIM TO FAME First Gentile to become a Christian

- A centurion was an officer in charge of one hundred men.

Cornelius was a Roman officer stationed with the occupying force in Caesarea. He was also a good man and a faithful follower of the Lord. The Jews, however, did not associate with Gentiles (non-Jews), so no one had told Cornelius about Jesus.

One day an angel appeared to Cornelius in a vision and told him to send for Peter. He immediately sent his servants to Joppa to find the apostle. Little did he know that at the same time, the Lord was also speaking to Peter, urging him to preach the gospel to the Gentiles. Cornelius's friends arrived at the house where Peter was staying and told him about Cornelius. The next day Peter went where Cornelius and all his family and friends were gathered. Peter told them about Jesus, and suddenly the Holy Spirit came upon the entire group. Peter was so amazed that he declared all of Cornelius's company should be baptized. Thus Cornelius showed Peter and all the apostles that the gospel was meant for people of all nations, not just the Jews.

STORY IN BIBLE 2 Chronicles 36; Ezra 1; Daniel 6

BORN Around 599 BC

NAME MEANING "Sun" (uncertain)

OCCUPATION King of Persia

RELATIVES Father—Cambyses

CONTEMPORARIES Daniel, Belshazzar

CLAIM TO FAME Brought the Israelites out of exile

- Wise king and great military leader
- Defeated Belshazzar and conquered Babylon
- Conquered Medes, Lydia, and Assyria to form the Persian Empire, the largest empire the world had yet seen
- Gave the Jews in Babylon permission to return to their homeland
- Ordered the rebuilding of the temple in Jerusalem
- Put Darius the Mede in charge of Babylon
- Although pagan, he was mightily used by the Lord to rescue His people from slavery
- His rule was prophesied by Isaiah three hundred years before

DANIEL — LION TAMER

STORY IN BIBLE Book of Daniel

BORN Around 621 BC in Jerusalem

NAME MEANING "God Is My Judge"

OCCUPATION Minister to kings of Babylon and Persia

CONTEMPORARIES Shadrach, Meshach, Abednego, Nebuchadnezzar, Belshazzar, Darius the Mede, Cyrus the Great

CLAIM TO FAME Stayed faithful to the Lord while serving pagan kings

- Was a teenager when Judah was conquered by Babylon
- Taken to Babylon by King Nebuchadnezzar
- Given a high position in the king's palace
- Named changed to Belteshazzar ("may Bel protect his life")
- Became Nebuchadnezzar's closest adviser
- Wrote the book of Daniel

STRENGTHS
- Known for his intelligence, wisdom, and purity
- Interpreted dreams and visions
- Prophesied about future events, including the end times

Despite the fact that he worked for pagan kings most of his life, Daniel never stopped worshiping the Lord. Often, this caused him problems. When he first arrived as a captive in Babylon with his three friends, he refused to eat the rich meats of the king's table. His overseer was certain the king would punish him if Daniel and his friends looked weak or sickly from only eating vegetables, but God strengthened their bodies so they appeared stronger and healthier than the other servants.

Then there was the time when the other ministers caught him praying to the Lord (which was against the law). They told the king, who was forced to throw Daniel into a den of lions as punishment. The king was upset because he really liked Daniel. He ran to the den early the next morning to discover that Daniel was still alive. God had sent angels to shut the mouths of the lions, and Daniel had survived.

Throughout his long life, Daniel managed to serve his masters faithfully while also serving the Lord. Although he never saw his homeland again, Daniel prayed continually for the Lord to show mercy to his people. God answered his prayer by eventually returning the Jewish people to Israel.

DID YOU KNOW?

Daniel had several encounters with angels, including Gabriel.

DAVID THE GIANT KILLER

STORY IN BIBLE 1 and 2 Samuel

BORN Around 1040 BC

NAME MEANING "Beloved One"

OCCUPATION Second king of Israel

RELATIVES Father—Jesse. Wives—Abigail, Michal, and Bathsheba (among others). Sons—Amnon, Absalom, Solomon, among others. Daughter—Tamar.

CONTEMPORARIES Samuel, Nathan, Jonathan, King Saul

CLAIM TO FAME Israel's second and greatest king

DID YOU KNOW?

As a boy, David played music that would calm King Saul's demons.

- Born in Bethlehem, same as Jesus
- Youngest of eight sons of Jesse
- Wrote almost half of the psalms (songs)
- Designed and planned the future temple

STRENGTHS

- Greatest king of Israel
- A man after God's own heart
- Great warrior and musician
- Listed in the ancestry of Jesus

WEAKNESSES

- Couldn't escape his sinful nature
- Committed adultery and murder
- Disobeyed God in taking a census
- Did not discipline his own children

David was just a shepherd boy when he volunteered to kill the Philistine giant Goliath. He was small, and although good-looking and "ruddy," he had no battle experience. He didn't even own a set of armor! No one thought he had a chance. But as a shepherd, he had fought lions and bears to protect his sheep, and he was not afraid of Goliath. All it took was one stone thrown from a shepherd's sling—and God's power—to beat the unbeatable giant and win the battle.

It was the first of many victorious battles for David. He became such a famous warrior that King Saul grew insanely jealous and tried repeatedly to kill him. Although God had already anointed David as the next king, he had to go into hiding in fear for his life. It took nearly twenty years before David finally sat on the throne.

David was always successful against his enemies in battle. But there was one enemy he couldn't quite over-come: his own desires. Those desires drove David away from God's will. In a tragic turn of events, he committed adultery and murder.

Still, David was a man "after God's own heart." He was faithful, courageous, and obedient to the Lord in a way King Saul never was. When David's sin was pointed out to him by the brave prophet Nathan, David made a full confession and repented. God forgave him. He never returned to his glory days, and he spent the rest of his life under attack by members of his own family. But his reign paved the way for the true King, born of his line in his hometown of Bethle-hem: Jesus the Messiah.

DEBORAH
A WORKING MOM

STORY IN BIBLE   Judges 4–5

BORN   Around 1360 BC

NAME MEANING   "Bee"

OCCUPATION   Judge and prophetess

RELATIVES   Husband—Lappidoth

CONTEMPORARIES   Barak, Sisera

CLAIM TO FAME   Led the Israelites to victory against the Canaanites

DID YOU KNOW?

Deborah sat under a palm tree to deliver her judgments.

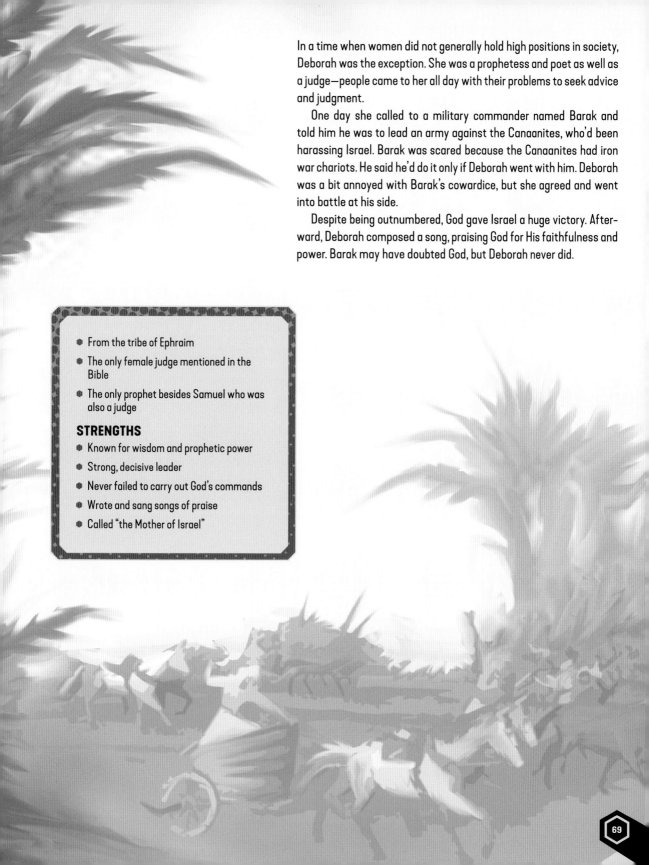

In a time when women did not generally hold high positions in society, Deborah was the exception. She was a prophetess and poet as well as a judge—people came to her all day with their problems to seek advice and judgment.

One day she called to a military commander named Barak and told him he was to lead an army against the Canaanites, who'd been harassing Israel. Barak was scared because the Canaanites had iron war chariots. He said he'd do it only if Deborah went with him. Deborah was a bit annoyed with Barak's cowardice, but she agreed and went into battle at his side.

Despite being outnumbered, God gave Israel a huge victory. Afterward, Deborah composed a song, praising God for His faithfulness and power. Barak may have doubted God, but Deborah never did.

- From the tribe of Ephraim
- The only female judge mentioned in the Bible
- The only prophet besides Samuel who was also a judge

STRENGTHS
- Known for wisdom and prophetic power
- Strong, decisive leader
- Never failed to carry out God's commands
- Wrote and sang songs of praise
- Called "the Mother of Israel"

DELILAH
A WOMAN ON A MISSION

STORY IN BIBLE Judges 16

BORN Around 1100 BC

NAME MEANING "Dangling Curls"

CONTEMPORARY Samson

CLAIM TO FAME Betrayed Samson by discovering the source of his strength

- Beautiful woman from Sorek with whom the judge Samson fell in love
- The only woman in Samson's story who is named
- Tasked by the Philistine leaders to find the source of Samson's strength so they could defeat him
- Cajoled Samson into telling her the secret, which was that if his hair was cut, he would lose his strength
- Had Samson's head shaved while he was asleep
- Was paid at least 1,100 pieces of silver for her service

STORY IN BIBLE Judges 3

BORN Around 1300 BC

NAME MEANING "Little Calf"

OCCUPATION King of Moab

CONTEMPORARIES

Ammonites, Amalekites, Ehud

CLAIM TO FAME Killed by a left-handed assassin

- King of the Moabites, a tribe descended from Moab, the son of Lot
- Raised up by God to teach the Israelites a lesson because they were doing evil
- Conquered Jericho with the help of the Ammonites and the Amalekites

When the people of Israel were oppressed by the Moabites and cried out to the Lord, He raised up a man named Ehud from the tribe of Benjamin to rescue them. Ehud's task was to assassinate the Moabite king Eglon. Ehud went to the king to deliver the tribute the Israelites owed to him. Because Ehud was left-handed, his sword was strapped to his right thigh, so the king's guards didn't notice it. Ehud delivered the tribute and then left—but he went back and informed the king that he had a secret message from God. Eglon was in his "upstairs room," which was probably a bathroom. Ehud went in while Eglon was sitting on his "throne" and thrust his sword into the king's gut. But King Eglon was so fat that the sword disappeared in his enormous stomach! Ehud couldn't retrieve his sword, so he just ran, locking the door behind him. When Eglon's ministers found the door locked, they decided not to disturb him while he was relieving himself. Therefore, Eglon died, his guts spilling onto the floor. Ehud went on to lead a revolt against Moab that set Israel free for eighty years.

ELI

GOOD PRIEST, BAD DAD

- Priest of the sanctuary at Shiloh
- A judge of Israel
- Devout and sincere, but weak and indulgent
- Scolded Hannah when he thought she was drunk
- Blessed Hannah when he learned she was praying desperately for a child
- Raised Hannah's son Samuel and taught him how to be a priest
- Recognized that Samuel had a special gift for prophecy at a young age
- Did nothing to correct his own wicked and corrupt sons
- Was told by the Lord his sons would die on the same day
- Both sons were killed while carrying the ark of the covenant into battle against the Philistines. The ark was lost.
- When he heard what happened, Eli—98 years old and blind—fell off his chair, broke his neck, and died.

STORY IN BIBLE 1 Samuel 1–4

BORN 1170 BC

NAME MEANING "Exalted"

OCCUPATION Priest

RELATIVES Sons—Hophni, Phinehas

CONTEMPORARIES Hannah, Samuel

CLAIM TO FAME Raised and taught Samuel

STORY IN BIBLE Luke 1

BORN Around 40 BC near Galilee

NAME MEANING "God Is My Oath"

OCCUPATION Wife and mother

RELATIVES Husband—Zechariah. Son—John the Baptist.

CONTEMPORARY Mary

CLAIM TO FAME Mother of John the Baptist

Elizabeth was getting old and still childless, much to her sorrow, when her husband, Zechariah, received a message from an angel: she would become pregnant and give birth to a son (John the Baptist), who would prepare the people for the coming of the Lord. Despite her age, Elizabeth did become pregnant. When her cousin Mary came to visit her several months later, the child in Elizabeth's belly leaped for joy. Elizabeth, filled with the Holy Spirit, confirmed what the angel had told Mary—she would be the mother of the Messiah.

ELIJAH | MIRACLE MAN

STORY IN BIBLE 1 Kings 17–19; 2 Kings 2

BORN Around 900 BC

NAME MEANING "The Lord Is My God"

OCCUPATION Prophet

CONTEMPORARIES King Ahab, Queen Jezebel, Elisha, priests of Baal

CLAIM TO FAME Took care of God's business, and God took care of him

- Often came to blows with King Ahab and Queen Jezebel
- Known for dramatic demonstrations and speeches
- Performed many miracles, including raising a boy from the dead, multiplying a jug of oil, and parting the Jordan River
- Mentored Elisha, who took over his ministry
- Was taken to heaven in a fiery chariot
- Appeared with Moses and Jesus on the mount of transfiguration scene of the New Testament

STRENGTHS
- Wise and faithful prophet
- Not afraid to speak truth to the king

WEAKNESSES
- Tended to complain a lot
- Was a loner
- Fled in fear from Jezebel

A prophet's life in the days of the kings was not an easy one. Elijah's main job was giving King Ahab bad news, so he wasn't very popular at court. After he told the king there would be three years with no rain, he ended up living by a brook in the middle of nowhere, all alone. Yet God took care of him, sending ravens to feed him morning and evening.

At the end of that drought, Elijah came out of seclusion to challenge Queen Jezebel's pagan priests. Jezebel had been killing God's priests and destroying true worship of the Lord, so Elijah challenged the priests of Baal to a showdown on Mount Carmel. Two altars were built, one for Baal and one for the Lord. The prophets of each would ask for their god to set fire to their sacrifices. The priests of Baal couldn't do it, but Elijah's God was different. Even after His altar was doused with water, God sent such a huge fire from heaven that it burned up not only the sacrifice but the entire altar and all the water too. Then Elijah ordered the deaths of all 450 priests of Baal.

That wasn't the end of Elijah's trouble. Jezebel was out to kill him, and Elijah found himself once again in the desert, alone, afraid, dejected, and depressed. Yet God took care of him, even sending angels to bring him food. A short time later, God gave him something he didn't even realize he needed: a friend.

ELISHA | ELIJAH TIMES TWO

STORY IN BIBLE 1 Kings 19; 2 Kings 1–13

BORN Around 880 BC near Galilee

NAME MEANING "My God Is Salvation"

OCCUPATION Farmer and prophet

RELATIVES Father—Shaphat

CONTEMPORARIES Elijah, King Jehoram, Joram, Jehoshaphat

CLAIM TO FAME Carried on Elijah's work

DID YOU KNOW?

Elisha used a few loaves of bread to feed a crowd, just as Jesus would do hundreds of years later.

Elisha often gets mixed up with his mentor, Elijah, because they were close associates, their names sound the same, and they did many similar miracles. But whereas Elijah had been dramatic and fiery, Elisha was pretty calm and quiet. Elijah was a loner, and Elisha was a people person. Elijah lived in the desert, and Elisha lived in a community of others. Yet both were effective in doing God's will.

Probably the most famous story about Elisha concerns bears. One day Elisha was walking toward Bethel when a group of young men started taunting him. This was not just an insult; it was a total rejection of the Lord and His anointed prophets. Elisha put a curse on the young men, and two bears came out of the woods and attacked them.

Once, the king of Syria sent a whole army to kill Elisha because he kept giving away the king's secret plans to the Israelites. Elisha's servant woke up to see the city surrounded. He was terrified. But Elisha prayed that God would open his eyes, and suddenly, the servant saw what Elisha saw: an even bigger army of horses and chariots of fire sent from God to protect them.

Elisha did many miracles, including making salty water drinkable and making poisonous food good to eat. He is the only prophet known to have performed a miracle after his death, when a corpse tossed into his tomb came back to life when it touched his bones.

- Fairly wealthy landowner
- Called to be Elijah's companion and successor
- Less dramatic than Elijah
- Requested a "double share" of Elijah's spirit when they parted
- Received Elijah's cloak when Elijah was taken away in a fiery chariot
- Prophesied for more than fifty years
- Repeated several of Elisha's miracles, including parting the Jordan River, multiplying jugs of oil, and raising a boy from the dead
- Advised several kings of Israel in political and military battles
- Cured the Syrian general Naaman of leprosy

STRENGTHS
- Powerful prophet
- Miracle worker
- Known for helping poor and powerless people

ELYMAS

THE FALSE PROPHET

STORY IN BIBLE Acts 13

BORN First century AD

NAME MEANING "Wise One"

OCCUPATION Sorcerer

CONTEMPORARIES Paul, Barnabas, John

CLAIM TO FAME Struck blind for opposing the gospel

Elymas may be the Arabic name of Bar-Jesus, a Jewish false prophet in the service of the proconsul Sergius Paulus of Cyprus. He was sometimes referred to as "Magus," meaning sorcerer. When Paul, Barnabas, and John, led by the Holy Spirit, came to preach to the proconsul about Jesus, Elymas opposed their teaching and tried to keep his master away from the faith.

Paul saw immediately that Elymas was filled with deceit and called him a "son of the devil." Then Paul declared that Elymas would be struck blind—and he was. Because of this, the proconsul declared his faith in Jesus.

STORY IN BIBLE Genesis 5

BORN Unknown

NAME MEANING "Dedicated"

OCCUPATION Prophet

RELATIVES Father—Jared. Son—Methuselah.

CLAIM TO FAME Walked with God

- Seventh in the line of Adam
- Walked with God
- Lived 365 years
- Great-grandfather of Noah
- Didn't die but was "taken into heaven"
- Mentioned in Hebrews as one of the heroes of the faith
- Son, Methuselah, was the oldest person recorded in the Bible, living to be 969 years old

ESAU | *JACOB'S HAIRY TWIN*

STORY IN BIBLE Genesis 25–28; 33

BORN Around 2000 BC

NAME MEANING "Hairy"

OCCUPATION Huntsman

RELATIVES Father—Isaac. Mother—Rebekah. Brother—Jacob.

CLAIM TO FAME Sold his birthright for a bowl of stew

- Also known as Edom, which means "red," for his coloring
- Very hairy, as his name says
- Twin brother to Jacob but considered the firstborn
- Loved to hunt
- Unaware that Jacob and his mother, Rebekah, were plotting to take his inheritance from him
- Gave his birthright to Jacob in exchange for a bowl of stew
- Had his father's blessing stolen from him by Jacob
- Vowed to kill Jacob, who was forced to flee
- Forgave Jacob years later when the two met again
- Married Canaanite women
- Established the tribe of the Edomites (traditional enemies of Israel), who were conquered by Israelites during the conquest of Canaan

Book of Ezekiel

Around 620 BC

"The Strength of God"

Priest and prophet

Father—Buzi

Daniel, Jeremiah, Nebuchadnezzar

Prophesied Jerusalem's fall and its future restoration

- Descended from priestly family of Zadok
- Raised in Jerusalem
- Age twenty-five when captured and taken to Babylon
- Wife died during the exile
- Prophesied about the coming destruction of Jerusalem, which occurred about five years after his exile
- Acted out his prophecies in very bizarre ways, as directed by God
- Some of his prophecies included eating scrolls, burning his own hair, and lying on his side for a year, cooking barley cakes over a manure fire.
- Had a vision of dry bones rising up from the desert, signifying the Lord would bring His people back to their homeland one day

ESTHER
A QUEEN FOR SUCH A TIME AS THIS

STORY IN BIBLE Book of Esther

BORN Around 500 BC

NAME MEANING "Star"

OCCUPATION Queen of Persia

RELATIVES Cousin—Mordecai. Father—Abihail. Husband—Xerxes.

CONTEMPORARIES Haman

CLAIM TO FAME Saved the Jewish race from a holocaust

DID YOU KNOW?
The Festival of Purim still celebrates Esther's action in saving the Jewish people.

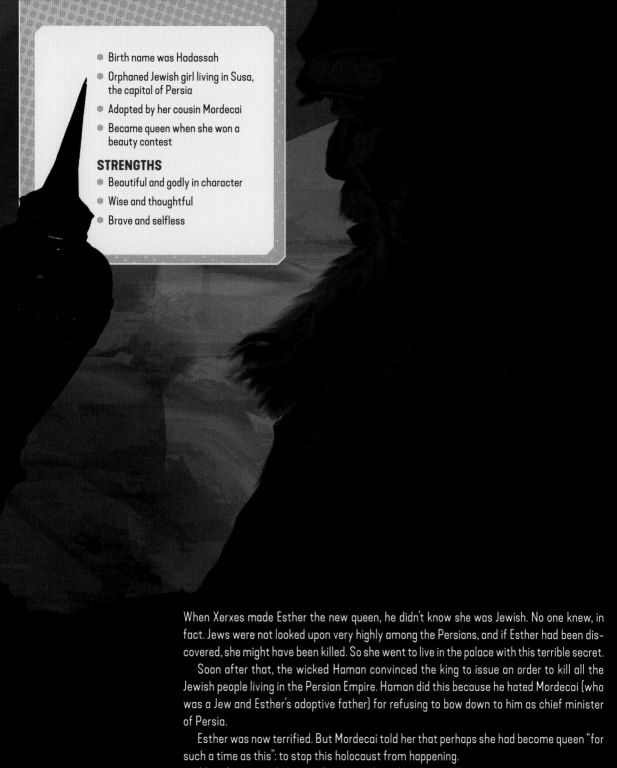

- Birth name was Hadassah
- Orphaned Jewish girl living in Susa, the capital of Persia
- Adopted by her cousin Mordecai
- Became queen when she won a beauty contest

STRENGTHS

- Beautiful and godly in character
- Wise and thoughtful
- Brave and selfless

When Xerxes made Esther the new queen, he didn't know she was Jewish. No one knew, in fact. Jews were not looked upon very highly among the Persians, and if Esther had been discovered, she might have been killed. So she went to live in the palace with this terrible secret.

Soon after that, the wicked Haman convinced the king to issue an order to kill all the Jewish people living in the Persian Empire. Haman did this because he hated Mordecai (who was a Jew and Esther's adoptive father) for refusing to bow down to him as chief minister of Persia.

Esther was now terrified. But Mordecai told her that perhaps she had become queen "for such a time as this": to stop this holocaust from happening.

After fasting and praying for strength and guidance, she came up with a courageous plan to go before the king. Her plan not only saved her people but also caused Haman to be hanged on the very gallows he had built for Mordecai.

EVE | *THE FIRST WOMAN*

STORY IN BIBLE Genesis 1–3

BORN Created from Adam's rib in the garden of Eden, before 4000 BC

NAME MEANING "Life-giving"

RELATIVES Husband—Adam. Children—Cain, Abel, Seth, and many more.

CLAIM TO FAME Was tempted by the serpent and ate the forbidden fruit

- First woman
- Called "mother of all the living"
- Lived in the garden of Eden
- Adam called her "woman" and then "Eve" after the fall

STRENGTH
- Helper and companion to Adam

WEAKNESSES
- Easily deceived by the serpent
- Did not take responsibility for her choice

DID YOU KNOW?

Adam named her Eve.

Eve is best known for the first sin. She was living a blissful life in the garden of Eden when a crafty serpent appeared and talked her into eating the fruit of the tree of the knowledge of good and evil, which God had forbidden. The serpent convinced Eve that nothing bad would happen (as God had said) and that she would be like a god herself, knowing good and evil. Eve took the bait. She ate the fruit and then gave some to Adam too.

The Lord was not pleased. Adam and Eve had broken the only rule He had given them. Adam blamed Eve. Eve blamed the serpent.

The Lord cursed Adam and Eve and then forced them to leave the garden of Eden forever, posting cherubim and a flaming sword at the entrance so they could not return.

The Lord also cursed the serpent and said the offspring of Eve would crush his head. This was a reference to Jesus' defeat of Satan one day in the future. (Although the serpent is not called Satan in this story, he certainly fits all the criteria.)

After leaving the garden of Eden, Eve then began to have many children, living up to her name. Cain, her firstborn, murdered Abel, her secondborn. It was a rough start for the first family, yet Eve would still become the "mother of all the living."

EZRA | THE REFORMER

STORY IN BIBLE Book of Ezra

BORN Around 480 BC

NAME MEANING "Help"

OCCUPATION Priest and scribe

CONTEMPORARIES Artaxerxes (king of Persia), Nehemiah

CLAIM TO FAME Led the return of the Jews out of exile

- Descendant of Aaron
- Lived in Persia
- A scribe (a student of God's laws and commandments)
- Was dismayed to see that the Jews remaining in Jerusalem were still worshiping idols
- Instituted religious reforms
- Read the entire Torah (first five books of the Bible) to all the people
- Demanded that Jews married to foreigners get divorces
- Set the example of piety and dedication to the Lord

HAGAR

STORY IN BIBLE Genesis 16; 21

BORN Around 2100 BC

NAME MEANING "Stranger"

OCCUPATION Servant

RELATIVES Son—Ishmael

CONTEMPORARIES Abraham, Sarah

CLAIM TO FAME The mother of Ishmael

- Egyptian bondservant to Sarai (later Sarah), the wife of Abram (later Abraham)
- Enlisted by Sarai to bear a son for Abram, as Sarai was barren
- Became disrespectful to Sarai, who treated her harshly
- Fled to the desert, where an angel appeared and told her to return to Sarai, promising she would have a son named Ishmael, a man "like a wild donkey"
- Cast into the desert with Ishmael after Sarah's son, Isaac, was born
- Rescued by God, who told her Ishmael would be the father of a great nation (later called the Ishmaelites)

GABRIEL | GOD'S MESSENGER

STORY IN BIBLE Daniel 8–9; Luke 1

NAME MEANING "Strong Man of God"

OCCUPATION Archangel

CONTEMPORARY Michael

CLAIM TO FAME Brought news of Jesus' coming to the world

- Described as the "guardian angel of Israel"
- Appeared to Daniel to reveal the meaning of his visions
- Appeared to Zechariah to bring news of the birth of John the Baptist
- Appeared to Mary to tell her she would give birth to the Messiah

STRENGTHS

- Messenger of the Lord
- Stands in the presence of God
- Supernatural being with ability to appear to humans and speak to them

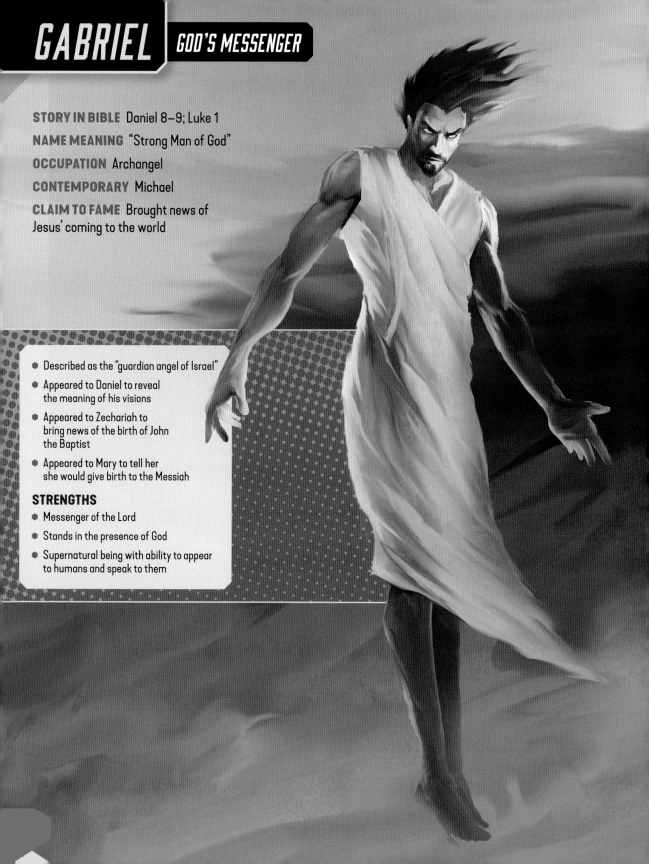

Gabriel is one of only two angels called by name in the Bible, the other being Michael.

The word *angel* actually means "messenger"—so it's really like a job description. Gabriel is mentioned once in the Old Testament and twice in the New Testament, bringing important messages from God to humans. He appeared in human form, but he still seemed to be somewhat terrifying.

Angels are only one kind of spiritual being in the heavenly realms. Others are seraphim and cherubim (which both have wings). Angels can't usually be seen in the human realm because they are spiritual beings without bodies. However, like Gabriel, angels can show up as humans, and the actual humans don't even realize it. In fact, Hebrews says, "Don't neglect to show hospitality, for by doing this some have welcomed angels as guests without knowing it" (13:2).

DID YOU KNOW?
Angels do not have wings, but some other heavenly beings are described as having wings.

GIDEON | VALIANT WARRIOR

STORY IN BIBLE Judges 6–8

BORN Around 1230 BC in Canaan

NAME MEANING "Slasher, Destroyer"

OCCUPATION Farmer turned warrior and judge

RELATIVES Father—Joash. Sons—Abimelech, Jotham.

CLAIM TO FAME Defeated the Midianites with only 300 men

- From the tribe of Manasseh
- Lived in Canaan after the conquest
- Won a great victory against a Midianite army
- Declined the demands of the people to become king
- Fifth judge of Israel
- Made an ephod (a garment or a statue) from the gold he received after the battle
- The people began to worship the ephod rather than the Lord
- Listed as a hero of the faith in Hebrews

STRENGTHS
- Willingness to do God's will
- Unafraid to ask the Lord for confirmation
- Became a great warrior and military strategist

WEAKNESSES
- Gave in to fear at first
- Doubted God's plan in choosing him to lead

DID YOU KNOW?

Gideon was nicknamed Jerubbaal ("May Baal Deal with Him") after he destroyed his family's altar to Baal.

When an angel appeared to Gideon and said, "The LORD is with you, valiant warrior," Gideon certainly didn't look like one. In fact, he was hiding in a winepress, trying to thresh his wheat out of sight of Midianites who were sweeping the countryside, stealing crops and killing people.

God wanted Gideon to raise an army to defeat the Midianites. Gideon wasn't so sure about this plan. But after the LORD provided undeniable proof, Gideon accepted the mission.

Thousands of warriors showed up to fight, but God didn't want them to think they could defeat the Midianites in their own strength. So He whittled the army down to three hundred.

With so few men, Gideon came up with an ingenious plan. He had spied on the Midianites and heard that one of them had a dream that they would be defeated. Gideon took advantage of their fear. He staged a night attack, surrounding the Midianite camp on three sides. He had his men blow trumpets and break jars containing torches, all the while shouting, "A sword for the LORD and for Gideon!" The fire and the noise threw the Midianites into total panic, and they started killing each other. With God's help, Gideon, who once hid in fear from the enemy, was victorious.

GOLIATH
THE BIG, UNFRIENDLY GIANT

STORY IN BIBLE 1 Samuel 17

BORN Around 1100 BC in Gath

NAME MEANING "Noticeable"

OCCUPATION Philistine warrior

CONTEMPORARIES David, King Saul

CLAIM TO FAME The mighty warrior defeated by a boy with a sling

DID YOU KNOW?

Goliath had four brothers, so that might be the reason David carried four extra stones in his pocket.

- From Gath, a place known for harboring giants (the Anakim)
- More than nine feet tall
- Armor weighed one hundred twenty-five pounds
- Iron spear weighed fifteen pounds
- Champion of the Philistine army

STRENGTHS
- Great warrior
- Physical power

WEAKNESSES
- Overconfident
- Bully

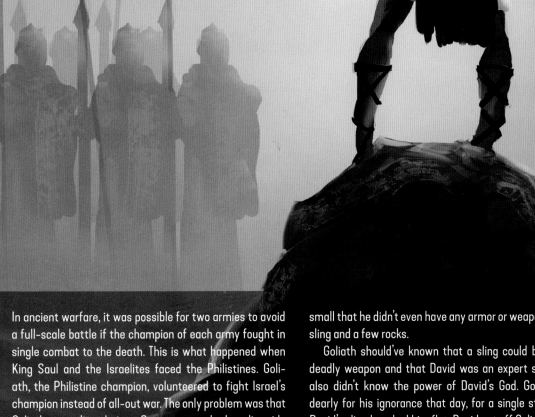

In ancient warfare, it was possible for two armies to avoid a full-scale battle if the champion of each army fought in single combat to the death. This is what happened when King Saul and the Israelites faced the Philistines. Goliath, the Philistine champion, volunteered to fight Israel's champion instead of all-out war. The only problem was that Goliath was a literal giant. So no one on the Israelite side wanted to fight him, for it meant certain death.

But then a young shepherd boy named David stepped forward. Goliath thought David was a joke. David was so small that he didn't even have any armor or weapons, just a sling and a few rocks.

Goliath should've known that a sling could be quite a deadly weapon and that David was an expert slinger. He also didn't know the power of David's God. Goliath paid dearly for his ignorance that day, for a single stone from David's sling knocked him flat. David cut off Goliath's head with the giant's own sword and took his head and his armor as a trophy. From that day on, David became a mighty hero of Israel, and Goliath a defeated foe.

HAM
NOAH'S WAYWARD SON

STORY IN BIBLE Genesis 5–10

BORN Unknown

NAME MEANING "Hot"

OCCUPATION Assistant zookeeper and vineyard worker

RELATIVES Father—Noah. Brothers—Shem, Japheth. Sons—Cush, Mizraim, Put, Canaan.

CLAIM TO FAME His son, Canaan, was cursed for Ham's sin

- Second son of Noah
- One of eight people on the ark during the great flood
- Committed a great sin against his father after returning to land
- Noah put a curse on Ham's son Canaan, saying he would be ruled by his brothers.
- Established his dynasty in Egypt
- Descendant Nimrod became a powerful ruler and founder of the city of Babylon (Babel)
- The curse on Ham was fulfilled when the Canaanites, descendants of Ham, were conquered by the Israelites.

STORY IN BIBLE Book of Esther

BORN Around 500 BC

NAME MEANING "Magnificent"

OCCUPATION Court official

RELATIVES Father—Hammedatha

CONTEMPORARIES Esther, Mordecai, King Ahasuerus

CLAIM TO FAME Plotted to exterminate the Jews

- An Agagite, possibly related to the Amalekites, traditional enemies of the Jews
- Chief minister or vizier to King Xerxes
- Hated Mordecai for disrespecting him
- Conceived a plot to have all Jews in the Persian Empire killed
- Saw his plot thwarted by Queen Esther, who happened to be Jewish
- The king learned of his plot and hanged him on the gallows he had built for Mordecai.
- His ten sons were also killed.
- During the Festival of Purim, people today sometimes write Haman's name on the soles of their shoes to express contempt.

HANNAH | WOMAN OF GRACE

STORY IN BIBLE 1 Samuel 1

BORN Around 1140 BC

NAME MEANING "Grace"

OCCUPATION Wife, mother

RELATIVES Husband—Elkanah. Son—Samuel, additional children.

CLAIM TO FAME The mother of the prophet Samuel

- From the tribe of Ephraim
- One of two wives of Elkanah, but especially loved by him
- Distraught because she had no children, unlike Elkanah's other wife
- Prayed for a child so passionately that the priest Eli thought she was drunk
- Gave birth to Samuel a year later
- Dedicated Samuel to God and brought him back to Eli when he was three years old to be raised at the synagogue
- Visited Samuel every year and brought him a new coat
- Had five more children
- Sang a prophetic song praising God for His faithfulness and grace in answering her prayer

HEZEKIAH

STORY IN BIBLE 2 Kings 18–20; 2 Chronicles 29–32

BORN Around 750 BC

NAME MEANING "The Lord Is My Strength"

OCCUPATION Twelfth king of Judah

RELATIVES Father—Ahaz. Son—Manasseh.

CONTEMPORARIES Isaiah, Sennacherib (Assyrian ruler)

CLAIM TO FAME Saved Judah from Assyrian conquest

- Son of wicked King Ahaz
- Destroyed pagan shrines and restored temple worship
- Prayed regularly
- The northern kingdom of Israel was conquered by Assyria during his reign
- Prepared Jerusalem for Assyrian attack by strengthening the walls, raising towers, and digging a tunnel to bring water into the city
- Assured by Isaiah that the Lord would defeat his enemy
- Angel of the Lord destroyed all 185,000 Assyrian troops
- Hezekiah got sick, but he prayed, and God gave him fifteen more years to live.
- Unwisely showed off his treasures to Babylonian visitors
- Warned by Isaiah that one day those treasures would be carried off to Babylon, a prophecy that came true a century later

HEROD THE GREAT

STORY IN BIBLE Matthew 2

- Ruled Judea 37–4 BC
- Was given the title "King of the Jews" by the Romans
- Rebuilt the temple of Jerusalem
- Started many other large building projects
- Effective and ruthless ruler
- Had ten wives
- Had many of his own family members killed
- Had all boys under two years old in Bethlehem murdered after hearing the prophecies of the wise men concerning Jesus
- While claiming to worship the one true God, also worshiped pagan gods
- Died of maggot-infested gangrene

HEROD ANTIPAS

STORY IN BIBLE Matthew 14

- Ruled 4 BC–AD 39
- Brutal and ruthless like his father
- Married his brother's wife
- Had John the Baptist imprisoned for denouncing his marriage
- Jesus referred to him as "that fox"
- Mocked Jesus during His trial
- Was later exiled by the Emperor Caligula

HERODIAS

STORY IN BIBLE Matthew 14, Mark 6, Luke 3

- Born around 9 BC
- Granddaughter of Herod the Great, sister to Herod Agrippa I
- Wife of both brothers Herod Philip and Herod Antipas
- Hated John the Baptist for denouncing her marriage to her husband's brother
- When Herod Antipas offered her daughter, Salome, a gift for dancing at his birthday party, she told her daughter to ask for the head of John the Baptist on a platter.

HEROD AGRIPPA I

STORY IN BIBLE Acts 12

- Ruled AD 37–44
- Persecuted the early church
- Had the apostle James executed and arrested Peter, who was later freed from prison by an angel
- Consumed with worms and died because he allowed himself to be worshiped like a god

HEROD AGRIPPA II

STORY IN BIBLE Acts 26

- Ruled AD 50–100
- The last and least brutal of the Herodians
- Had an audience in Caesarea with Paul, who spoke of Jesus and the resurrection
- Hinted he might have been persuaded to become a Christian
- Was king when Jerusalem was destroyed by Rome in AD 70

HOSEA

A PROPHET WITH A TOUGH JOB

Book of Hosea

Around 780 BC

"The Lord Saves"

Prophet

Father—Beeri. Wife—Gomer.

CONTEMPORARIES King Jeroboam II, King Hezekiah

CLAIM TO FAME His life demonstrated God's plan for Israel

Lived when the northern kingdom of Israel was about to be conquered by Assyria

Faithful to God

Called to marry an unfaithful woman named Gomer to demonstrate Israel's sin of worshiping other gods

Every time Gomer left him for other men, the Lord told Hosea to bring her back, signifying that although Israel would be exiled, the Lord would bring His people home again.

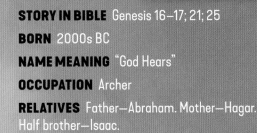

THE NOT-FORGOTTEN SON   *ISHMAEL*

STORY IN BIBLE Genesis 16–17; 21; 25

BORN 2000s BC

NAME MEANING "God Hears"

OCCUPATION Archer

RELATIVES Father—Abraham. Mother—Hagar. Half brother—Isaac.

CLAIM TO FAME Abandoned by his father, but God protected him

- Son of Abraham and the Egyptian servant Hagar
- Was kicked out of Abraham's house along with his mother because he was teasing his half brother, Isaac
- Nearly died under a bush in the desert but was rescued by God's angel
- God promised Hagar He would make Ishmael's descendants into a great nation.

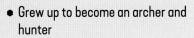

- Grew up to become an archer and hunter
- Settled in the Wilderness of Paran
- Married an Egyptian woman
- Helped bury his father
- Fathered twelve sons who became leaders of tribes
- Died at the age of 137

ISAAC | *THE BOY WHO LIVED*

STORY IN BIBLE Genesis 21–27

BORN 2000s BC

NAME MEANING "Laughter"

OCCUPATION Wealthy sheepherder

RELATIVES Father—Abraham. Mother—Sarah. Half brother—Ishmael. Wife—Rebekah. Sons—Jacob, Esau.

CLAIM TO FAME Used by God to test Abraham's faith

- The fulfillment of God's promise to Abraham
- A loving though sometimes weak-willed husband and father
- Favored his older son, Esau
- Was tricked into giving his blessing to his younger son, Jacob

STRENGTHS
- Obedient son
- Worshiped the Lord

WEAKNESSES
- Did not lead his family well or manage family strife

DID YOU KNOW?

Sarah gave birth to Isaac when she was ninety years old, which might be why she named him "laughter."

Isaac was the child promised to Abraham and Sarah, although the promise was not fulfilled until Abraham was one hundred years old. Isaac didn't go on adventures like his father. He seems to have led a quiet life as a wealthy sheepherder. The only real excitement was when his father, on orders from God, took him up to a mountain to sacrifice him when he was still pretty young. His father even asked him to carry the wood that would be used for the sacrifice. Isaac, who didn't know anything about what was to happen, asked his father where the animal for the sacrifice was. Abraham replied that God would provide it.

What was Isaac thinking as he lay on the altar, his father holding a knife over his head? We aren't told. We know only that an angel stopped Abraham, and the Lord provided a ram instead. Abraham's faith and obedience had been tested, but so had Isaac's. He didn't jump up and run away or even question his father's action. He obeyed the Lord and his father.

Isaac's life was one of obedience. He married a beautiful girl named Rebekah, who bore twin sons, Jacob and Esau. Unfortunately, Isaac did not seem aware of the rivalry between his sons or the scheming of his wife until it was too late.

ISAIAH

THE PROPHET OF THE KING OF KINGS

STORY IN BIBLE Book of Isaiah; 2 Kings 19–20

BORN Around 710 BC

NAME MEANING "The Lord Is Salvation"

OCCUPATION Prophet

RELATIVES Father—Amoz. Wife—Unnamed.
Sons—Shear-jashub, Maher-shalal-hash-baz.

CONTEMPORARIES Kings Uzziah, Jotham, Ahaz, Hezekiah

CLAIM TO FAME Foretold the coming of Jesus

DID YOU KNOW?

According to Jewish writings, Isaiah died when he was sawn in two by the wicked King Manasseh.

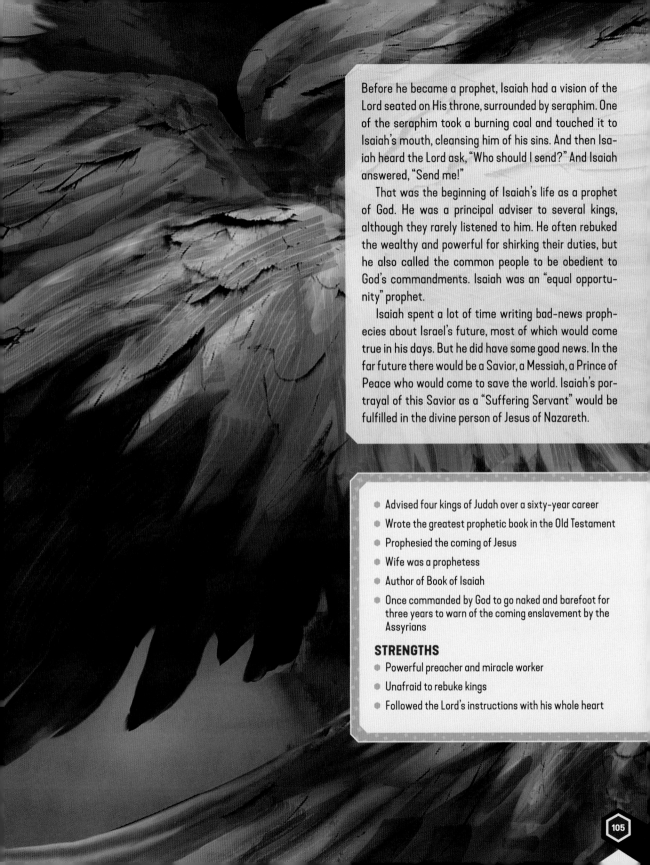

Before he became a prophet, Isaiah had a vision of the Lord seated on His throne, surrounded by seraphim. One of the seraphim took a burning coal and touched it to Isaiah's mouth, cleansing him of his sins. And then Isaiah heard the Lord ask, "Who should I send?" And Isaiah answered, "Send me!"

That was the beginning of Isaiah's life as a prophet of God. He was a principal adviser to several kings, although they rarely listened to him. He often rebuked the wealthy and powerful for shirking their duties, but he also called the common people to be obedient to God's commandments. Isaiah was an "equal opportunity" prophet.

Isaiah spent a lot of time writing bad-news prophecies about Israel's future, most of which would come true in his days. But he did have some good news. In the far future there would be a Savior, a Messiah, a Prince of Peace who would come to save the world. Isaiah's portrayal of this Savior as a "Suffering Servant" would be fulfilled in the divine person of Jesus of Nazareth.

- Advised four kings of Judah over a sixty-year career
- Wrote the greatest prophetic book in the Old Testament
- Prophesied the coming of Jesus
- Wife was a prophetess
- Author of Book of Isaiah
- Once commanded by God to go naked and barefoot for three years to warn of the coming enslavement by the Assyrians

STRENGTHS
- Powerful preacher and miracle worker
- Unafraid to rebuke kings
- Followed the Lord's instructions with his whole heart

JACOB | THE GRABBER

STORY IN BIBLE Genesis 25–49

BORN Around 2000 BC

NAME MEANING "Heel Grabber" or "Cheater"

OCCUPATION Sheepherder

RELATIVES Father—Isaac. Mother—Rebekah. Brother—Esau. Grandfather—Abraham. Wives—Leah, Rachel. Sons—Reuben, Simeon, Levi, Judah, Dan, Naphtali, Gad, Asher, Issachar, Zebulun, Joseph, Benjamin. Daughter—Dinah.

CLAIM TO FAME Founded the twelve tribes of Israel

- Esau's twin, although Jacob was born second and, therefore, considered younger
- Preferred indoor activities, whereas Esau liked to hunt
- Took advantage of Esau twice to cheat him out of his inheritance
- Had twelve sons who became the leaders of the twelve tribes of Israel

STRENGTHS
- Prosperous businessman and sheepherder
- Eventually followed God's laws and worshiped Him alone

WEAKNESSES
- Selfish and deceptive
- Initially followed God as long as he got what he wanted

Jacob's name says it all. He started life as a thief and deceiver. He was named Jacob because he grabbed his brother Esau's heel as he was being born. He also grabbed Esau's birthright and the blessing of their father through deception. Esau was so angry that Jacob had to get out of town quickly.

Many years later, after he'd married, made a fortune, and had a bunch of kids, Jacob decided to return home. He was preparing to meet his brother again (and probably imagining Esau still wanted to kill him) when a mysterious man showed up and started a wrestling match. Jacob and the man wrestled all night long. Then the man touched Jacob's hip and threw it out of joint. Jacob knew then that he had been wrestling with the Lord Himself. He stopped fighting and clung to the "man," saying he would not let go until the "man" blessed him. That night, God changed Jacob's name to Israel, which means "wrestles with God."

Jacob is very much like us. He started out trying to do everything his own way, grabbing what he wanted. He had to learn the hard way that instead of wrestling with God, we should be clinging to Him.

DID YOU KNOW?

Jacob walked with a limp after wrestling all night with God.

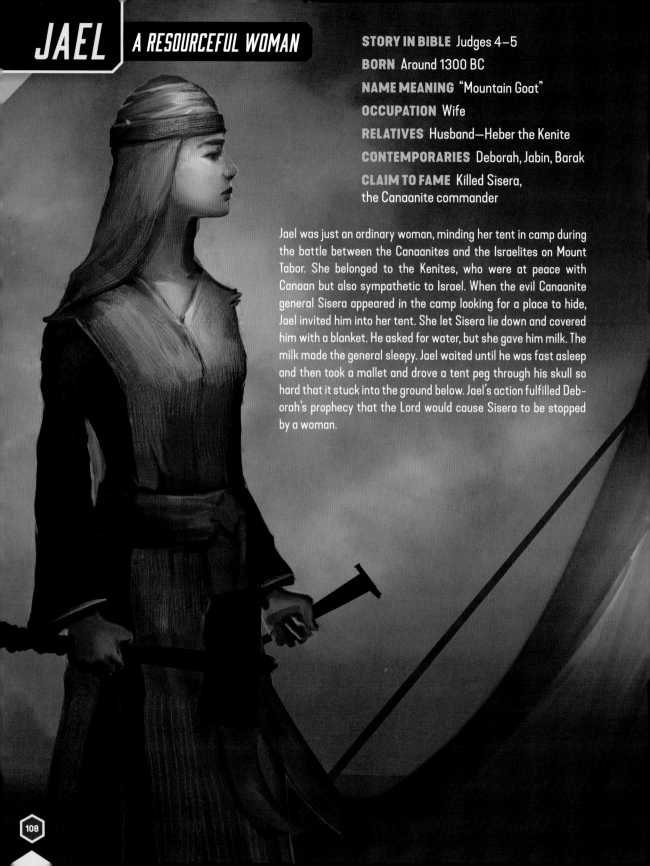

JAEL

A RESOURCEFUL WOMAN

STORY IN BIBLE Judges 4–5

BORN Around 1300 BC

NAME MEANING "Mountain Goat"

OCCUPATION Wife

RELATIVES Husband—Heber the Kenite

CONTEMPORARIES Deborah, Jabin, Barak

CLAIM TO FAME Killed Sisera,
the Canaanite commander

Jael was just an ordinary woman, minding her tent in camp during the battle between the Canaanites and the Israelites on Mount Tabor. She belonged to the Kenites, who were at peace with Canaan but also sympathetic to Israel. When the evil Canaanite general Sisera appeared in the camp looking for a place to hide, Jael invited him into her tent. She let Sisera lie down and covered him with a blanket. He asked for water, but she gave him milk. The milk made the general sleepy. Jael waited until he was fast asleep and then took a mallet and drove a tent peg through his skull so hard that it stuck into the ground below. Jael's action fulfilled Deborah's prophecy that the Lord would cause Sisera to be stopped by a woman.

A FATHER WITH FAITH | JAIRUS

STORY IN BIBLE Mark 5; Luke 8

BORN First century AD

NAME MEANING "He Enlightens"

OCCUPATION Synagogue ruler

RELATIVES Wife—Unnamed. Daughter—Unnamed.

CONTEMPORARIES Jesus, Peter

CLAIM TO FAME Believed Jesus could heal his daughter

Jairus was a synagogue ruler in Capernaum in Jesus' time, which meant he was in charge of the synagogue's maintenance and services. Most synagogue rulers did not approve of Jesus' teaching, but Jairus was different. When his daughter became deathly ill, Jairus went to Jesus and begged Him to heal her. Jesus agreed. But on the way to Jairus's house, a servant appeared and said the girl was dead and there was no need for Jesus. Jesus told the distraught Jairus, "Don't be afraid. Only believe."

Jesus went to the house and saw the dead girl lying on her bed. He told everyone to leave except a select few and then commanded the girl to get up. And she did! Jesus then told her to eat something to prove to her parents she wasn't a ghost.

Jairus's daughter was one of three resurrections Jesus would perform. But He told Jairus not to tell anyone what he had seen—yet.

JAMES | THE BROTHER OF JESUS

STORY IN BIBLE Book of James

BORN First century AD

NAME MEANING Form of Jacob, "Supplanter"

OCCUPATION Church elder

RELATIVES Half-brother—Jesus. Mother—Mary. Father—Joseph.

CLAIM TO FAME Head of the church at Jerusalem

- Younger brother of Jesus
- Didn't believe Jesus was the Messiah at first and thought Jesus might have been insane.
- Met with Jesus after the resurrection and then believed He was truly the Son of God
- Wrote the book of James
- Chairman of first church council in which it was decided Gentiles didn't have to follow all the Jewish laws to become Christians
- Martyred for his faith, probably by stoning

STORY IN BIBLE Matthew 4; Mark 1; Luke 5

BORN First century AD

NAME MEANING Form of Jacob, "Supplanter"

OCCUPATION Fisherman, apostle

RELATIVES Brother—John. Father—Zebedee. Mother—Salome.

CLAIM TO FAME One of the twelve apostles

- Older brother of the apostle John
- Wealthy, successful family
- Fisherman on the Sea of Galilee with John, Peter, and Andrew
- Helped to bring in a huge load of fish (one of Jesus' miracles)
- One of Jesus' inner circle, along with Peter and John
- He and John were nicknamed "Sons of Thunder" by Jesus because of their boldness and hot tempers.
- Wanted to rain down fire on a village that refused to welcome Jesus
- Asked if he could sit beside Jesus when He took His throne
- Present at the resurrection of Jairus's daughter and the transfiguration
- The first apostle to be martyred—killed with a sword by order of Herod Agrippa

JEHORAM | *JUDAH'S BAD BOY*

2 Kings 8; 2 Chronicles 21

Around 880 BC

"The Lord Has Exalted"

Fifth king of Judah

Father—Jehoshaphat. Wife—Athaliah (daughter of Ahab and Jezebel). Sons—Ahaziah, plus several unnamed.

Elijah, Joram (king of Israel)

One of Judah's most evil kings

- Not to be confused with the Joram of Israel, who reigned during the same time (sometimes their names were swapped). In fact, Joram is the shortened version of Jehoram.

- Eldest son of King Jehoshaphat

- Reversed all the good things done by his father

  - Killed all six of his brothers as well as some of the princes of Israel to secure his throne

    - Rebuilt the altars to Baal due to the influence of his idolatrous wife

- Ignored the warnings of the prophet Elijah that judgment would fall upon his house

- His possessions and most of his family were taken away and killed by invading Philistine and Arabian armies

- Was struck by the Lord with a horrific disease in which his intestines literally fell out of his body over a two-year period

- Died after eight years of rule but was denied burial in the tombs of the kings

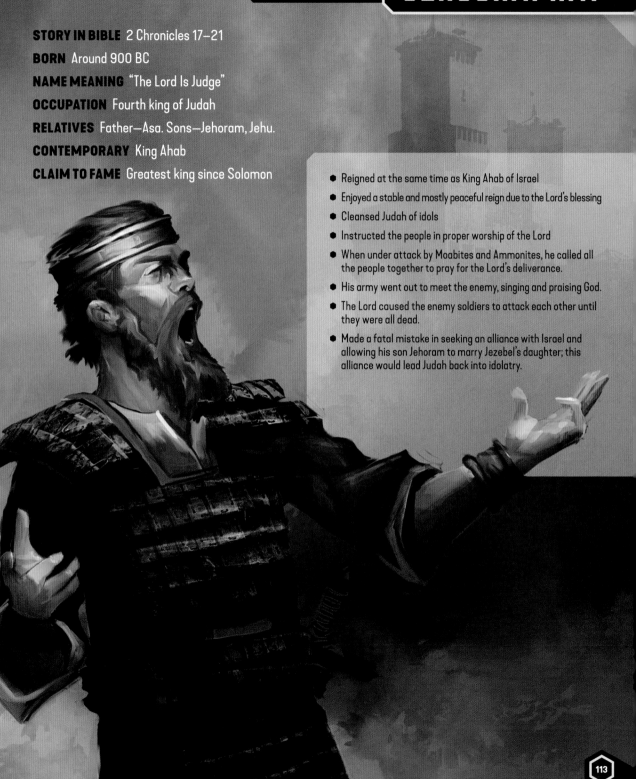

JEHOSHAPHAT

STORY IN BIBLE 2 Chronicles 17–21

BORN Around 900 BC

NAME MEANING "The Lord Is Judge"

OCCUPATION Fourth king of Judah

RELATIVES Father—Asa. Sons—Jehoram, Jehu.

CONTEMPORARY King Ahab

CLAIM TO FAME Greatest king since Solomon

- Reigned at the same time as King Ahab of Israel
- Enjoyed a stable and mostly peaceful reign due to the Lord's blessing
- Cleansed Judah of idols
- Instructed the people in proper worship of the Lord
- When under attack by Moabites and Ammonites, he called all the people together to pray for the Lord's deliverance.
- His army went out to meet the enemy, singing and praising God.
- The Lord caused the enemy soldiers to attack each other until they were all dead.
- Made a fatal mistake in seeking an alliance with Israel and allowing his son Jehoram to marry Jezebel's daughter; this alliance would lead Judah back into idolatry.

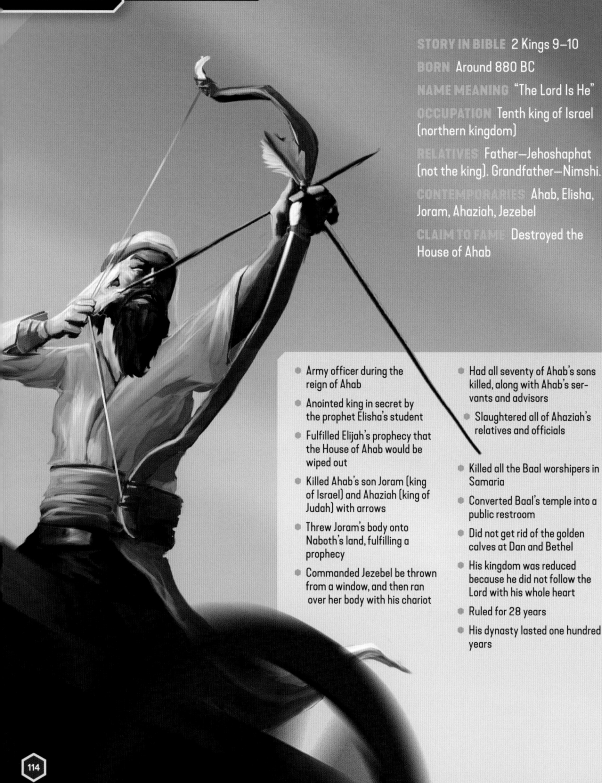

JEHU | THE BLOODY KING

STORY IN BIBLE 2 Kings 9–10

BORN Around 880 BC

NAME MEANING "The Lord Is He"

OCCUPATION Tenth king of Israel (northern kingdom)

RELATIVES Father—Jehoshaphat (not the king). Grandfather—Nimshi.

CONTEMPORARIES Ahab, Elisha, Joram, Ahaziah, Jezebel

CLAIM TO FAME Destroyed the House of Ahab

- Army officer during the reign of Ahab
- Anointed king in secret by the prophet Elisha's student
- Fulfilled Elijah's prophecy that the House of Ahab would be wiped out
- Killed Ahab's son Joram (king of Israel) and Ahaziah (king of Judah) with arrows
- Threw Joram's body onto Naboth's land, fulfilling a prophecy
- Commanded Jezebel be thrown from a window, and then ran over her body with his chariot

- Had all seventy of Ahab's sons killed, along with Ahab's servants and advisors
- Slaughtered all of Ahaziah's relatives and officials
- Killed all the Baal worshipers in Samaria
- Converted Baal's temple into a public restroom
- Did not get rid of the golden calves at Dan and Bethel
- His kingdom was reduced because he did not follow the Lord with his whole heart
- Ruled for 28 years
- His dynasty lasted one hundred years

JEPHTHAH

STORY IN BIBLE Judges 11–12

BORN Around 1250 BC

NAME MEANING "God Opens"

QUALIFICATION Military leader and judge

RELATIVES Father—Gilead

CLAIM TO FAME Delivered Israel from the Ammonites

- Rejected by his brothers because he had a different mother

- Ran into the wilderness, where he gathered a band of fierce fighting men

- Became so well known as a warrior that his townspeople asked him to defend them against the Ammonites.

- Agreed to lead his people if they would make him ruler

- Made a foolish vow before the battle that he would give to the Lord whatever or whoever met him at the door of his house when we returned home

- Won the battle, but when he went home it was his daughter who came out of the house first

- Was despondent because he had to fulfill his vow and offer his daughter to the Lord

- Became a judge of Israel and ruled for six years

- Named a Hero of the Faith in Hebrews

JEREMIAH | THE WEEPING PROPHET

DID YOU KNOW?

Jeremiah is known as the "Weeping Prophet" because he suffered terribly for his dark prophecies.

STORY IN BIBLE Books of Jeremiah, Lamentations

BORN Around 650 BC

NAME MEANING "May the Lord Exalt"

OCCUPATION Prophet

RELATIVES Father—Hilkiah

CONTEMPORARIES Kings Josiah, Jehoiakim, Jehoiachin, Zedekiah, Nebuchadnezzar (king of Babylon)

CLAIM TO FAME Foretold the conquest of Jerusalem

Jeremiah was the most abused prophet in the Bible. Because of his radical preaching against idolatry and false prophets, Jeremiah was slandered, imprisoned, exiled, put in stocks, and thrown into a well and left to die. There were even murder plots against him. When Jeremiah tried to warn King Jehoiakim about the coming conquest by Babylon, the king burned Jeremiah's scrolls rather than listen to him.

Jeremiah prophesied for more than forty years to four different kings. None of them heeded his warnings.

When finally the Babylonian king Nebuchadnezzar surrounded Jerusalem, Jeremiah advised King Zedekiah to surrender. Zedekiah put him in prison for treason. The siege lasted over two years until the people inside the city walls were killing each other for food. In the end, Jerusalem surrendered.

But Jeremiah also prophesied that God had plans for His people, not for harm, but for their ultimate good. That promise came true with the birth of God's Son, Jesus.

- Son of a priest who lived in the territory of Benjamin
- Told by God he had been chosen before he was born
- Called to ministry at a young age
- Told God he couldn't be a prophet because he didn't know how to speak. God told him He would provide the words.
- Prophesied that the captivity of Israel would last seventy years.
- Author of Jeremiah and Lamentations
- Offered a home in Babylon by Nebuchadnezzar, but refused
- Was taken to Egypt by a group of Jews and never heard from again

STRENGTHS
- Willing to endure persecution to proclaim God's word
- Powerful preacher and writer

WEAKNESSES
- At first did not trust his calling to be God's prophet

JEROBOAM | A DIVISIVE KING

STORY IN BIBLE 1 Kings 11–14; 2 Chronicles 10–11

BORN Around 950 BC in Ephraim

NAME MEANING "He Who Contends"

OCCUPATION First king of northern kingdom

RELATIVES Father—Nebat. Son—Abijah.

CONTEMPORARIES Solomon, Rehoboam, Ahijah the prophet

CLAIM TO FAME Split the kingdom in two

- Not born of a royal line
- Supervisor of tribe of Ephraim, appointed by King Solomon
- Helped rebuild the defenses of Jerusalem
- Told by the prophet Ahijah that he would rule ten tribes of Israel because the Lord was splitting the kingdom due to Solomon's idolatry
- Fled to Egypt when Solomon tried to have him killed
- As leader of the rebellion, tried to negotiate with Solomon's son Rehoboam but was rebuffed
- Crowned king of the ten tribes, thereafter known as the northern kingdom of Israel
- Instead of leading his people into true worship of the Lord, plunged them deeper into idolatry by creating golden calves at Bethel and Dan
- Because of his idolatry, the Lord told him his son would die and his ancestral line would be destroyed

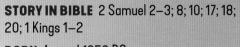

STORY IN BIBLE 2 Samuel 2–3; 8; 10; 17; 18; 20; 1 Kings 1–2

BORN Around 1050 BC

NAME MEANING "The Lord Is Father"

OCCUPATION Military commander

RELATIVES Mother—Zeruiah (David's sister). Brothers—Abishai, Asahel.

CONTEMPORARIES David, Absalom, Abner

CLAIM TO FAME David's top general

- Cunning and ruthless commander of David's armies
- Fiercely loyal to David
- Won the battle to secure David's throne
- Killed his rival Abner, who had killed Joab's brother Asahel
- Killed Amasa, another rival for his position
- Against David's orders, killed David's rebellious son Absalom (as he hung by his hair from a tree)
- Backed Adonijah rather than Solomon as David's successor
- Before he died, David ordered Joab to be executed for his murders
- Killed by his successor Benaiah beside the altar in the tabernacle (tent of meeting)

STORY IN BIBLE Matthew; Mark; Luke; John

BORN Around 5 BC in Bethlehem

NAME MEANING "The Lord Is Salvation"

OCCUPATIONS Craftsman, rabbi, traveling preacher

RELATIVES Adoptive Father—Joseph. Mother—Mary. Brother—James, among others.

CONTEMPORARIES King Herod, Pontius Pilate, the disciples including Peter, James, John.

CLAIM TO FAME Son of God, Savior of the world, Messiah

DID YOU KNOW?

On the night of His arrest, Jesus prayed with such grief that His sweat was like drops of blood.

- The promised Messiah
- Descended from the line of David
- Fulfills more than one hundred Old Testament prophecies about the Messiah, including the "Suffering Servant" in Isaiah
- Began His public ministry at the age of thirty
- Name is pronounced *Yeshua* in Hebrew
- Spoke Aramaic

- Called Himself "the bread of life." His birthplace, Bethlehem, means "House of Bread."
- First miracle was changing water into wine at a wedding.
- Called God "Abba," which means something like "Daddy"
- Raised three people from the dead
- Although sinless, convicted of a capital crime and punished by death on a Roman cross
- Was raised from the dead on the third day

- Spent forty days with His followers after His resurrection before ascending into heaven
- Only one of Jesus' miracles (besides His own resurrection) is in all four gospels: the feeding of the 5,000

STRENGTHS

- Sinless, perfect
- Miracle worker
- Raised from the dead
- Forgave those who killed Him

The whole Bible is really about Jesus. He was God's final answer to the sin and suffering of the world. In Jesus' own words: "For God loved the world in this way: He gave his one and only Son, so that everyone who believes in him will not perish but have eternal life" (John 3:16).

The four Gospels tell Jesus' story from different points of view. Matthew shows us Jesus the Jewish Messiah and King of kings and details how all the prophecies of the Old Testament pointed to His coming to the world. Mark shows us Jesus the man of action and miracle worker. Luke, a Gentile (non-Jewish) doctor, shows us Jesus as the good shepherd—His humanity, compassion, and care for His flock, both Jew and Gentile. John, one of Jesus' disciples, shows us Jesus the Son of God, fully man and fully divine.

Jesus performed many miracles and taught people about God. He traveled long and far with his twelve friends, the disciples. At first He was extremely popular, due to all the miracles, but by the end of His life most people deserted Him.

Jesus was the most important person who ever lived. He never sinned, yet He died on a Roman cross like a criminal, taking the punishment for the sins of the world so that those who believe in Him can be with Him forever.

JEZEBEL | THE QUEEN OF MEAN

STORY IN BIBLE 1 Kings 16–2 Kings 9

BORN Around 900 BC

NAME MEANING "Where Is the Prince?"

OCCUPATION Queen of northern kingdom of Israel

RELATIVES Husband—King Ahab. Father—King Ethbaal of Sidon. Sons—Joram, Ahaziah. Daughter—Athaliah.

CONTEMPORARIES Elijah, Jehu

CLAIM TO FAME Tried to destroy all the priests of Israel

DID YOU KNOW?

Jezebel was eaten by dogs after her death, fulfilling Elijah's prophecy.

The most wicked queen in Israel's history wasn't Jewish. In fact, she hated the Jewish religion and had most of God's prophets and priests murdered. Only a hundred survived, hiding in caves. She installed her own pagan religion in Israel and got her husband the king to turn from God and worship Baal.

But God was still on the throne, and He put a stop to Jezebel. First, Elijah the prophet destroyed all her priests and prophets in one spectacular miracle on Mount Carmel. Later on, the new king of Israel, Jehu, killed both Jezebel's sons and then Jezebel herself, in one of the most gruesome deaths in the entire Bible, which had been foretold by Elijah.

As bad as Jezebel was, her daughter, Athaliah, would turn out to be even worse.

- From Sidon, a Phoenician city to the north of Israel (modern-day Lebanon)
- Married to King Ahab of Israel
- Had Naboth killed when he refused to give his land to the king
- Tried to have Elijah killed
- Died after being thrown out of a window and run over by a chariot

STRENGTHS
- Powerful and decisive queen

WEAKNESSES
- Worshiped pagan gods
- Led her husband and Israel astray
- Committed numerous murders
- Persecuted God's prophets

JOB | TROUBLED WITH A CAPITAL T

STORY IN BIBLE Book of Job

BORN Before 2000 BC

NAME MEANING "Where Is the Father?"

OCCUPATION Wealthy sheepherder

RELATIVES Wife (unnamed). Many children (unnamed).

CONTEMPORARIES Three friends—Eliphaz, Zophar, Bildad—and Elihu

CLAIM TO FAME Stayed faithful to God despite terrible suffering

- From Uz, near Midian, where Moses lived for forty years
- Story takes place before the nation of Israel existed

WEAKNESS
- Questioned God's goodness

STRENGTHS
- Very wealthy
- Generous and loving to his family
- Faithful to God despite intense suffering

Job was a righteous man who always walked in God's ways, even offering sacrifices in case one of his party-hard children accidentally insulted the Lord. God was pleased with Job. But one day a member of His divine council (called "satan" or "the adversary") asked for permission to test Job, to see if his faith was real or just the result of his happy, prosperous life. God gave permission. So the adversary caused all ten of Job's children to be killed in a storm and his flocks and herds to be destroyed. To make things even worse, Job came down with a terrible disease and was covered in painful boils.

Job was in such agony that he wanted to die. He questioned why God would allow this suffering to come upon him. Even Job's wife told him he should "curse God and die." When his three so-called friends arrived, they told him he must have done something really bad for God to punish him like this. Job didn't appreciate their input. "You are all miserable comforters," he said.

In the end, God himself spoke to Job through a violent storm. He reminded Job that He was God and Job was not. And just because Job didn't understand the reason for his suffering didn't mean there wasn't one. Job's steadfast faith through his trial was a victory for the kingdom of God. Eventually Job was restored to health and blessed with children once again.

DID YOU KNOW?

The book of Job is considered the oldest book in the Bible.

JOHN THE BAPTIST

WILD MAN

STORY IN BIBLE	Matthew; Mark; Luke; John
BORN	Around 6 BC in Judah
NAME MEANS	"The Lord Has Been Gracious"
OCCUPATION	Baptizer, prophet
RELATIVES	Father—Zechariah. Mother—Elizabeth. Cousin—Jesus.
CONTEMPORARIES	Herod Antipas, Herodias
CLAIM TO FAME	Announced the coming of the Messiah

DID YOU KNOW?

John dressed and acted so much like the prophet Elijah that many people thought he was Elijah reborn.

126

John lived in the desert, dressed in camel hair, and ate locusts and wild honey. Sounds a bit crazy, right? This was the guy that God had sent to proclaim the coming Messiah.

Like Jesus, John's birth came about by a miracle of God. He was set apart for the mission of getting people to repent and prepare for the coming Messiah.

When Jesus came to him to be baptized, John declared that Jesus was the Lamb of God and that John was not worthy to baptize him. But when he did, he saw the heavens open and the Spirit of God descending upon Jesus.

As Jesus' ministry grew, John's began to wane. But he knew that was going to happen. He called himself a voice crying out in the wilderness, preparing the way of the Lord.

After his imprisonment by Herod Antipas, John seems to have wondered if Jesus really was the long-awaited Messiah. Jesus assured him that He was. Not long after, John was beheaded by Herod as a gift for his stepdaughter, Salome. Yet John had fulfilled his mission. He had prepared the way of the Lord.

- His birth was announced by the angel Gabriel, just like Jesus' birth
- Miraculous birth to an elderly couple who couldn't have children
- First prophet called by the Lord in four hundred years
- His coming was prophesied by Isaiah
- Baptized Jesus
- Imprisoned and beheaded by Herod Antipas for criticizing his marriage to Herod's brother's wife

STRENGTHS
- Fearless preacher, calling people to repent
- Uncompromising in his faith and lifestyle

WEAKNESSES
- Doubted Jesus was the Messiah after his imprisonment

JOHN | THE BELOVED DISCIPLE

STORY IN BIBLE Matthew; Mark; Luke; John; Acts; 1, 2, 3 John; Revelation

BORN First century AD

NAME MEANING "The Lord Has Been Gracious"

OCCUPATION Fisherman, apostle

RELATIVES Father—Zebedee. Mother—Salome. Brother—James.

CONTEMPORARIES Jesus, the disciples

CLAIM TO FAME Wrote the Gospel of John; 1, 2, 3 John; and Revelation

- In the fishing business with his brother James and friends Peter and Andrew
- A disciple of John the Baptist
- Jesus called John and James "Sons of Thunder"
- One of Jesus' inner circle, along with James and Peter
- The youngest apostle
- Sat next to Jesus at the Last Supper

- Witnessed the transfiguration
- The only apostle to be at the trial and crucifixion of Jesus
- Was entrusted with the care of Jesus' mother
- Along with Peter, took the lead in founding the early Church

STRENGTHS:
- Devoted to Jesus and stayed with Him until the end
- Powerful writer who penned five books of the New Testament

WEAKNESSES
- Tendency to angry outbursts
- Sometimes thought he was better than the other apostles

DID YOU KNOW?

In his gospel, John refers to himself in the third person as "the disciple Jesus loved."

John is often painted as Jesus' favorite apostle. He ended up living the longest—the only apostle who wasn't martyred for his faith. After Jesus went to heaven, John preached the gospel in Jerusalem and Samaria, despite being persecuted often. One time he and Peter were thrown in jail—and released by an angel. He wrote the fourth gospel of the New Testament, emphasizing Jesus' divine nature, His godhood,

and His love. John wrote over and over about love, telling people to love one another as Jesus had commanded.

For his unbridled preaching of Jesus as Lord, John was exiled to the island of Patmos, where he received a startling vision of the end times—the ultimate war in heaven when Satan stages his final rebellion. John wrote it all down in what is known as Revelation, the last book of the Bible.

JONAH
A WHALE OF A PROPHET

STORY IN BIBLE Book of Jonah

BORN 800s BC in Gath-hepher

NAME MEANING "Dove"

OCCUPATION Prophet

RELATIVES Father—Amittai

CONTEMPORARIES King Jeroboam II, Hosea, Amos

CLAIM TO FAME Swallowed by a big fish

- Hometown was very near Nazareth, where Jesus grew up
- Jesus compared Jonah's three days in the big fish to His own three days in the tomb
- Jonah was able to persuade the more than 120,000 citizens of Nineveh to repent
- Jonah is the only prophet to preach to people outside of the nation of Israel
- Nineveh was near Mosul in modern-day Iraq

STRENGTHS
- Devoted prophet of the Lord
- Powerful preacher

WEAKNESSES
- Tried to run away when God sent him to preach to Nineveh
- Was angry when God showed mercy on the people

Jonah was an obedient prophet of the Lord . . . until the Lord told him to go and preach in the great city of Nineveh.

Nineveh was the capital of Assyria, which was the nation that was trying to conquer Israel. Naturally, Jonah didn't want to go. He wanted Nineveh to be destroyed, not saved. So he hopped on a ship going in the opposite direction. But when a violent storm overtook the ship, Jonah knew he was the cause. He volunteered to go overboard to save the ship.

Jonah was promptly swallowed by a "great fish." He stayed in the fish's stomach for three days until he had a change of heart. When the fish vomited him up on the shore, Jonah then spent three days walking around Nineveh to deliver God's message. To his dismay, the people of Nineveh repented of their sins. God spared the city. Jonah was so upset that Nineveh wasn't destroyed that he asked God to kill him. But God spared Jonah too and taught him an important lesson about how He cares for the whole world.

DID YOU KNOW?
The whole body of a man in armor from the sixteenth century was once found in the stomach of a great white shark.

JONATHAN | FRIEND AND HERO

STORY IN BIBLE 1 and 2 Samuel

BORN Around 1050 BC

NAME MEANING "The Lord Has Given"

OCCUPATION Prince and Warrior

RELATIVES Father—Saul. Sisters—Michal, Merab. Son—Mephibosheth.

CONTEMPORARY David

CLAIM TO FAME Helped David escape King Saul

DID YOU KNOW?

Jonathan's victorious strategy for the battle of Michmash was successfully used in World War I at the exact same location.

- King Saul's son and heir
- Best friends with David
- His sister Michal became David's wife

STRENGTHS
- Courageous warrior
- Put others before himself
- Totally dependent on God
- Loyal to his father, King Saul

Of all the heroes of the Bible, there are few as good and true and faithful as Jonathan.

King Saul's eldest son was a mighty warrior and one of the bravest men who ever lived. He had defeated the Ammonites and the Philistines. Once he attacked a Philistine outpost on a cliff top at Michmash with only his armor-bearer, killing twenty men at once and sending the entire garrison running for their lives. He could do this because he believed wholeheartedly that God would be faithful and deliver him.

Yet Jonathan knew that it was David, not he, whom God had chosen to succeed his father. Instead of being jealous or angry, Jonathan became David's best friend. He protected David when King Saul turned against him and tried to kill him. In doing so he brought Saul's wrath upon himself. Yet Jonathan did not abandon his father either. He remained a loyal son and valiant captain in his army, eventually dying at his father's side in battle.

Matthew 27; Mark 15; Luke 23; John 19

Around 20 BC

"May He Add"

Elder, Member of Sanhedrin

Jesus, disciples, Nicodemus

Buried Jesus' body

- A wealthy man who genuinely sought the kingdom of God
- From Arimathea, a Judean town—the location is debated
- Member of Sanhedrin, the governing council of Jewish elders
- Followed Jesus in secret for fear of the Jews
- Argued against Jesus' execution
- Asked Pontius Pilate for Jesus' body after His death
- Took Jesus' body down from the cross, along with Nicodemus
- Buried Jesus in his own rock-cut tomb situated in a garden

JOSEPH

STORY IN BIBLE Matthew 1–2; Luke 3

BORN Around 30 BC

NAME MEANING "May He Add"

OCCUPATION Carpenter

RELATIVES Wife—Mary. Adopted son—Jesus.

CONTEMPORARY Herod the Great

CLAIM TO FAME Earthly father of Jesus

- In the ancestral line of David
- Lived in Nazareth, a hilltop town in northern Israel
- Never speaks a word in the Bible
- Probably made furniture and farm tools, as houses then were made of stone and earth
- Was told in a dream to marry Mary, even though she was already pregnant
- Took Mary to his family's hometown of Bethlehem to register for the census
- Was told in a dream to take Jesus and Mary to Egypt to escape Herod
- Is not mentioned at all after Jesus is about 12 years old

JOSEPH THE DREAMER

STORY IN BIBLE Genesis 37–50

BORN Around 1915 BC in Canaan

NAME MEANING "May He Add"

OCCUPATION Shepherd, slave, prime minister of Egypt

RELATIVES Father—Jacob. Mother—Rachel. Brothers—Reuben, Simeon, Levi, Judah, Dan, Naphtali, Gad, Asher, Issachar, Zebulun, Benjamin. Sister—Dinah. Wife—Asenath (Egyptian). Sons—Manasseh, Ephraim.

CLAIM TO FAME Saved Egypt and his own family from famine

DID YOU KNOW?
Moses brought Joseph's bones out of Egypt during the exodus.

- Eleventh of the twelve sons of Jacob
- Born to Rachel, Jacob's favored wife
- Famous for his "coat of many colors"
- After the conquest of Canaan, his tribe was split in two, named after his sons Manasseh and Ephraim
- Died at age 110

STRENGTHS

- Able to interpret dreams
- Great statesman and organizer
- Faithful to God
- Did not give in to temptation

WEAKNESSES

- Pride and arrogance got him into trouble

When he was young, Joseph dreamed he would be so great that his eleven brothers would bow down to him. His brothers weren't thrilled with that dream, so one day they sold him into slavery in Egypt.

Joseph became a slave in the household of an Egyptian businessman named Potiphar. He did well and earned Potiphar's favor until an unjust accusation landed him in prison for about thirteen years. But God had not forgotten Joseph. His gift for interpreting dreams eventually brought him to the attention of Pharaoh, who was so impressed that he made Joseph his second in command, tasked with preparing for a coming famine.

Joseph's careful planning kept Egypt from disaster when the rest of the world was starving. Then one day, Joseph's brothers came to him, begging for food. They didn't recognize the brother they'd sold into slavery years before. After testing them for a while, Joseph finally revealed himself and forgave them for what they had done to him, saying, "You meant it for evil, but God meant it for good."

After a joyful reunion, the whole family moved to Egypt. The Israelites stayed there for more than four hundred years until another pharaoh enslaved them and God came to their rescue once again.

JOSHUA THE KING SLAYER

STORY IN BIBLE Numbers and Joshua

BORN Around 1470s BC in Egypt

NAME MEANING "The Lord Is Salvation"

OCCUPATION Warrior, Leader of Israelites after Moses

RELATIVES Father—Nun. Sister—Rahmah. Brother—Eran.

CONTEMPORARIES Moses, Caleb

CLAIM TO FAME Conquered Canaan, the Promised Land

DID YOU KNOW?

Joshua once asked God to cause the sun and moon to stand still so he could finish a battle.

- Joshua's name is the Hebrew version of Jesus or Yeshua
- Moses' right-hand man. Took over after Moses' death.
- God often reminded Joshua to be courageous and strong
- Probably in his late sixties when he entered Canaan
- Fought thirteen battles
- Killed five Amorite Kings
- Defeated a total of thirty-one kings in his conquest

STRENGTHS
- Great military leader
- Trusted God and did everything He commanded
- Courageous warrior

Joshua was one of only two people who left Egypt and entered the promised land. He and Caleb had been with the spies who had gone to scout out the land God had given to the Israelites. They counseled Moses to invade according to God's instructions, but the others were too afraid. God was angry at the people's lack of faith and commanded that all who had left Egypt would die in the desert, except for Joshua and Caleb.

After Moses' death, Joshua took over command and led the conquest of Canaan. His first battle was his most famous, although he actually didn't do much fighting. At the walled-city of Jericho, a heavenly being appeared to Joshua and instructed him to carry out bizarre instructions that involved marching around the city seven times and blowing trumpets. If he did that, the messenger told him, the walls would fall down. Though it sounded impossible, Joshua carried out the orders faithfully, and the mighty walls of Jericho did come crashing down.

Joshua's life was one of unprecedented military success and unwavering faithfulness to God. Sadly, only a generation later, the Israelites would forget about the Lord's faithfulness and sink back into idolatry.

JOSIAH
THE IDOL SLAYER

2 Kings 22–23; 2 Chronicles 34–35

Around 650 BC

"The Lord Heals"

Fifteenth king of Judah

RELATIVES Father—Amon. Mother—Jedidah. Grandfather—Manasseh.

CONTEMPORARY Jeremiah

CLAIM TO FAME Restored the temple and destroyed idols

- Became king at age 8
- Father and grandfather were considered evil kings
- Set out to destroy all idol worship in Israel
- Burned the bones of deceased idol priests on their altars
- Had the neglected temple repaired and cleaned
- Found the neglected books of the Law (the first five books of the Bible)
- Was helped by Jeremiah in religious reforms
- Went into battle in disguise and was killed
- Had been told by a prophetess that he would die before Judah came under judgment by God
- Died at the age of 39 when he tried to stop an Egyptian army from passing through his kingdom

JUDAH

STORY IN BIBLE Genesis 29, 37, 38

BORN Around 1920 BC

NAME MEANING "Praise the Lord"

OCCUPATION Farmer

RELATIVES Father—Jacob. Mother—Leah. Brothers—Reuben, Simeon, Levi, Issachar, Zebulun, Joseph, Benjamin, Dan, Naphtali, Gad, Asher. Sister—Dinah. Sons—Er, Onan, Shelah. Daughter-in-law—Tamar.

CLAIM TO FAME Founded the tribe that produced David and Jesus

- Fourth of twelve sons of Jacob
- Often acted as leader and spokesman for the family
  - Convinced the other brothers to spare Joseph
  - Jacob prophesied that Judah was a "lion's cub" and would rule over the others
- Married a Canaanite woman
- God took the lives of two of his sons because they were evil in His sight
- Failed badly in his dealing with Tamar, his daughter-in-law
- His tribe became the largest in number and had the largest share of the land
- When Israel was split, the tribes of Judah and Benjamin became a separate kingdom

JUDAS ISCARIOT | *THE BETRAYER*

STORY IN BIBLE Matthew 26; Mark 14; Luke 22; John 18

BORN First century AD

NAME MEANING "To Praise"

OCCUPATION Apostle of Jesus, treasurer

RELATIVES Father—Simon Iscariot

CONTEMPORARIES Jesus, Peter, the other disciples

CLAIM TO FAME Betrayed Jesus to the Jewish leaders

Judas is the most complicated villain in the Bible. He was one of the twelve apostles who had followed Jesus faithfully for three years, and yet he betrayed Jesus for thirty pieces of silver, about $600 in today's money. Why did he do it? And why did Jesus, who knew what Judas was going to do, allow him to remain as a apostle?

Many reasons have been given through the years for Judas' betrayal. Luke and John both claim that Judas was heavily influenced by Satan. Another theory is that Judas betrayed Jesus hoping it would force Him to reveal His true nature and take over as king of the Jews. Or it could be that when Judas realized that Jesus wasn't going to be made king, and in fact the chief priests were looking to kill Him, he decided to take the money and run.

We don't know for sure. What we do know is Judas couldn't escape his own guilt. He could have asked for forgiveness, but instead he hanged himself on the very property that was later purchased with the thirty pieces of silver.

DID YOU KNOW?

Judas was replaced by Matthias as the twelfth apostle.

- One of the twelve apostles
- Treasurer for the disciples and often helped himself to the moneybag
- Complained when Mary poured perfume on Jesus' feet, claiming it should have been sold to help the poor
- Betrayed Jesus for thirty pieces of silver

STRENGTHS
- A loyal disciple until his betrayal
- Felt remorse for his action

WEAKNESSES
- Greedy, loved money
- Prideful and arrogant

LAZARUS | THE MAN WHO LIVED AGAIN

STORY IN BIBLE John 11

BORN First century AD

NAME MEANING "God Helps"

OCCUPATION Possibly farmer

RELATIVES Sisters—Mary, Martha

CONTEMPORAY Jesus

CLAIM TO FAME Raised from the dead by Jesus

Lazarus was a friend of Jesus who lived in Bethany, a few miles from Jerusalem. When he became ill, his sisters, Mary and Martha, sent for Jesus. But Jesus delayed His arrival until after Lazarus had died. He'd been dead for four long days when Jesus finally arrived. Mary and Martha were upset that Jesus had not come sooner. But Jesus had other plans. He went to the tomb where Lazarus was buried, had the stone rolled away, and commanded Lazarus to come out. A few minutes later, the stunned crowd saw Lazarus, still wrapped in strips of linen, walk out of the tomb! Many believed in Jesus after that, which made the Jewish leaders all the more determined to kill Him. Soon after, Lazarus held a banquet honoring Jesus, the man who had given him a second chance at life.

STORY IN BIBLE Genesis 29

BORN 1900s BC

NAME MEANING "Wild Cow"

OCCUPATION Wife, mother

RELATIVES Father—Laban. Sister—Rachel. Husband—Jacob. Sons—Reuben, Simeon, Levi, Judah, Issachar, Zebulun. Daughter—Dinah.

CLAIM TO FAME Jacob's wife

- Older daughter of Laban, Jacob's uncle
- Was considered not as pretty as her sister, Rachel
- Married Jacob against his will through her father's trickery
- Desired Jacob's love, which he never gave
- Learned to depend on the love of the Lord rather than her husband
- Gave birth to six of the twelve sons of Jacob
- Died before the family left for Egypt

LEGION | *THE DEMONIAC*

- A demoniac is a person possessed by demons
- "Legion" also refers to a large Roman military unit
- Removing demons from a person is called an exorcism

STORY IN BIBLE Mark 5; Luke 8

BORN First century AD

NAME MEANING "Multitude"

RELATIVES Unknown

CONTEMPORARY Jesus

CLAIM TO FAME Healed of demons by Jesus

He said his name was *Legion* because he was possessed by so many demons. He lived in tombs and was so violent he broke the chains used to restrain him. Day and night he howled, bruising himself with stones and tearing his clothes.

Until he met Jesus.

The demons knew exactly who Jesus was, and they were terrified. They begged Jesus to send them into some pigs that were feeding nearby. When Jesus gave them permission, they immediately left Legion and went into the pigs. The pigs went wild, raced down the hill to the sea, and drowned.

When people came out to see about the commotion, they found Legion perfectly calm, clothed, and in his right mind. Instead of being amazed and thankful, they were afraid. They told Jesus to leave their town. Legion wanted to go with Him, but Jesus told him to go back home and tell everyone what God had done for him.

LOT

STORY IN BIBLE Genesis 11–14; 19

BORN 2100s BC

NAME MEANING "Hidden"

OCCUPATION Sheepherder

RELATIVES Father—Haran. Uncle—Abraham. Wife—unnamed. Daughters—unnamed.

CLAIM TO FAME Lived in Sodom before it was destroyed

- Followed his uncle Abraham on his journey to Canaan
- Eventually separated from Abraham and moved to Sodom
- Became a leader in the city of Sodom, a wicked city near the Dead Sea
- Was captured by four kings who attacked Sodom and was rescued by Abraham
- Angels came to Sodom to warn Lot and his family to leave.
- Sodom was destroyed by the Lord with fire and "brimstone"—burning sulfur raining from the sky.
- Lot and his daughters escaped, but his wife "looked back" and was turned into a pillar of salt.
- That region is so salty that nothing can grow to this day.
- A pillar of salt resembling a woman stands in the region of the Dead Sea today.

LUKE | THE GOOD DOCTOR

STORY IN BIBLE Gospel of Luke; Acts of the Apostles

BORN First century AD

NAME MEANING "Light Giving" (uncertain)

OCCUPATION Physician, missionary

CONTEMPORARIES Paul, the apostles

CLAIM TO FAME Wrote the Gospel of Luke and Acts of the Apostles

- Not one of the original disciples
- The only writer of any book of the Bible who was a Gentile (non-Jew)
- Recorded the story of Jesus' birth, the Christmas story
- Excellent historian
- Luke's gospel emphasizes Jesus' care for the poor, women, children, and social outcasts. It contains the most stories about healing, perhaps because he was a doctor.
- He addressed both of his books to a mysterious person named "Theophilus." The name means "lover of God."
- Traveling companion of Paul the Apostle
- Chronicled Paul's missionary journeys

Acts 16

First century AD

"Native of Lydia" (uncertain)

Fabric merchant

Paul, Luke

Paul's first Gentile convert

- Lived in Philippi, on the coast of Greece
- Sold purple cloth, which was considered the color of wealth and royalty
- Very prosperous, head of her household
- Paul met her after receiving a vision that he was to go to Macedonia (Greece).
- Paul discovered Lydia with a group of women praying by a river.
- Lydia's home became Paul's base of operations in Philippi.
- Helped to establish the Philippian church, first Christian church in Europe
- Paul baptized her and her household, which probably included slaves.

MANASSEH | *THE MOST WICKED KING*

STORY IN BIBLE 2 Chronicles 33; 2 Kings 21

BORN Around 700 BC

NAME MEANING "God Has Made Me Forget"

OCCUPATION Thirteenth king of Judah

RELATIVES Father—Hezekiah. Mother—Hephzibah. Grandfather—Ahaz. Son—Amon.

CONTEMPORARY Isaiah

CLAIM TO FAME Plunged Judah into idolatry and wickedness

- Took the throne at age 12; reigned 55 years
- Put up a pagan shrine in the temple
- Sacrificed his own son to pagan gods
- Practiced witchcraft and fortune-telling and used mediums to commune with the dead
- Captured by the king of Assyria due to his disobedience; imprisoned in Babylon
- Repented for his sins; God forgave him
- Returned to Jerusalem, where he took down all of the idol altars he'd built
- Buried in his garden rather than with the kings of Judah
- His son Amon continued his wicked ways

STORY IN BIBLE   Acts 12; 15

BORN   First century AD

NAME MEANING   "Warlike"

OCCUPATION   Apostle

RELATIVES   Mother—Mary (not Jesus' mother). Cousin—Barnabas.

CONTEMPORARIES   Peter, Paul, Luke

CLAIM TO FAME   Wrote the Gospel of Mark

- John was his Jewish name; Mark was his Roman surname.
- Sometimes referred to in the Bible as "John"
- Disciple of Peter who spent much time at his mother's house teaching
- Wrote the action-packed Gospel of Mark
- Was the cause of Barnabas and Paul splitting up because Barnabas wanted to bring Mark along on another journey
- Patched things up with Paul who asked him to come visit him in prison
- He had some failures as a missionary, but his Gospel inspired millions to follow Jesus.
- The Gospel of Mark is the shortest of the four Gospels and was probably written first.

MARY | MOTHER OF THE MESSIAH

STORY IN BIBLE Matthew 1, 2, 13; Mark 3, 6; Luke 1–2; John 2; Acts 1; Revelation 12

BORN Around 20 BC in Nazareth

NAME MEANING "Strong-Willed"

OCCUPATION Wife, mother

RELATIVES Husband—Joseph. Cousin—Elizabeth. Children—Jesus, Joseph (sometimes Joses), James, Judas, Simon, daughters.

CLAIM TO FAME The mother of Jesus

- Was only person present at both Jesus' birth and death
- Sang a song often called "The Magnificat" praising God for His deliverance of her people
- Witnessed Jesus perform His first miracle—turning water into wine

STRENGTHS

- Courageous
- Obedient and willing to do whatever God asked of her
- Treasured everything in her heart

WEAKNESSES

- Unaware of Jesus' true identity and purpose

Mary was a teenager engaged to be married to Joseph when the angel Gabriel appeared to tell her she would have a son through the Holy Spirit, a Son who would be the Savior of the world. Although she didn't quite understand what the angel's news meant, she accepted God's pronouncement with grace and courage. She gave birth to Jesus and watched Him grow into a man filled with wisdom and supernatural power.

And years later she stood at the foot of a Roman cross and watched Him die.

This simple Jewish girl would become one of the most revered women in the history of the world, all because when God gave her an impossible task, she said, "Yes."

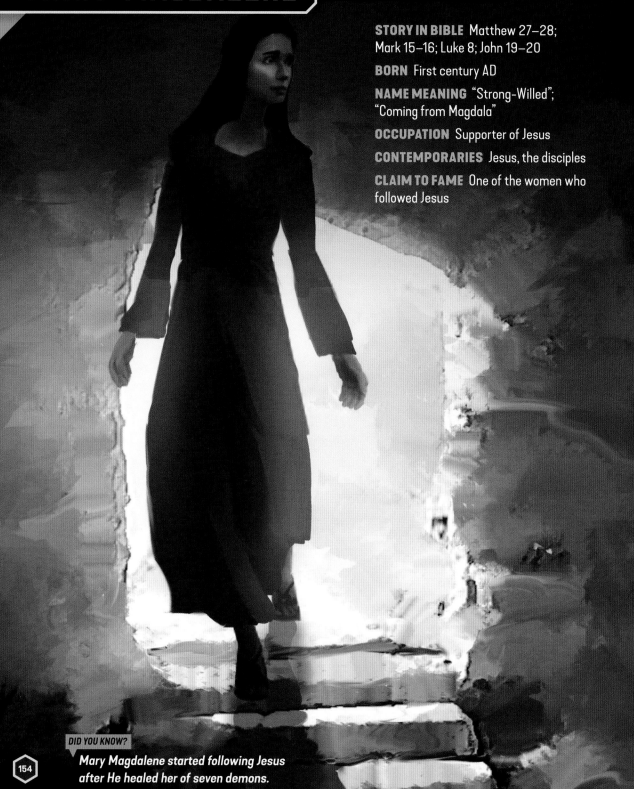

MARY MAGDALENE

DELIVERED FROM DEMONS

STORY IN BIBLE Matthew 27–28; Mark 15–16; Luke 8; John 19–20

BORN First century AD

NAME MEANING "Strong-Willed"; "Coming from Magdala"

OCCUPATION Supporter of Jesus

CONTEMPORARIES Jesus, the disciples

CLAIM TO FAME One of the women who followed Jesus

DID YOU KNOW?
Mary Magdalene started following Jesus after He healed her of seven demons.

We don't know anything about Mary Magdalene's family. She is never mentioned as anyone's wife or daughter or sister. She is just Mary of a town called Magdala, a fishing port in Galilee.

Mary Magdalene's family was Jesus. She was one of several women who followed Him, learned from Him, supported Him, and stood at the cross to watch Him die. When she went to the tomb early that Sunday morning to anoint His body per the Jewish custom, she found the stone rolled away and Jesus gone. She ran to tell the disciples. John and Peter came, investigated, and left. Mary stayed. As she stood weeping at the tomb's entrance, a voice said, "Woman, why do you weep?" She didn't know it was Jesus—she thought it was the gardener. Then He spoke her name: "Mary." And she knew her Lord was alive, just as He said He would be.

- One of Jesus' most devoted female followers
- Traveled with the disciples
- The first to discover the empty tomb, the first to see the risen Jesus, and the first to report what happened to the disciples

Strengths
- Extremely loyal to Jesus
- Stayed with Him until His death on the cross
- Had the financial means to support Jesus' ministry

Weaknesses
- Did not at first believe Jesus was risen from the dead

MARY AND MARTHA

STORY IN BIBLE Luke 10; John 11–12

BORN First century AD

NAME MEANING Mary—"Strong-Willed"; Martha—"Lady"

OCCUPATION Friends of Jesus

RELATIVES Brother—Lazarus

CONTEMPORARIES Jesus, the disciples

CLAIM TO FAME Good friends and benefactors of Jesus

STRENGTHS:

- Martha—Industrious, hard-worker
- Mary—Contemplative, eager to learn

WEAKNESSES

- Martha—Tendency to complain about having to do everything
- Mary—Tendency to not help out when needed

- Sisters living with their brother Lazarus in Bethany, a few miles from Jerusalem
- Jesus was a frequent guest in their home.
- Their brother, Lazarus, was resurrected by Jesus.
- At a feast in Jesus' honor, Mary poured pure nard on His feet and wiped it with her hair as a gesture of love and gratitude.

Mary and Martha were sisters, but they couldn't be more different. Martha was a fabulous homemaker and cook who was always serving Jesus when He came to visit. But instead of cooking and serving, Mary preferred to sit at Jesus' feet and listen to His words (which Jesus said was the better choice). Yet both women were devastated when Jesus failed to show up to heal their brother Lazarus who had become gravely ill.

When Jesus finally arrived, Lazarus had been dead four days. Jesus greeted the heartbroken sisters, who questioned Him as to why He hadn't come sooner. Jesus went to the tomb, ordered the stone rolled away, and commanded Lazarus to come out. Martha was at first horrified—she knew there would be a terrible smell. But then she and her sister saw their brother walk out of the tomb, alive and well!

DID YOU KNOW?

Mary anointed Jesus' feet with nard, also known as spikenard, an expensive essential oil from the East.

MATTHEW

THE TAX COLLECTOR WHO SAID YES

STORY IN BIBLE
Matthew 9; Mark 2;
Luke 5

BORN
First century AD

NAME MEANING
"Gift of God"

OCCUPATION
Tax collector

RELATIVES
Father—Alphaeus

CONTEMPORARIES
Jesus, the disciples,
Herod Antipas

CLAIM TO FAME
Wrote Gospel of
Matthew

- Also called Levi
- One of Jesus' twelve apostles
- Tax collector for Herod Antipas
- Tax collectors were hated by the Jews. Pharisees considered them the worst of sinners because they took money from their own people and often overcharged.
- Worked in Capernaum, collecting tariffs on goods that passed on the road between Damascus and the Mediterranean Sea
- Educated, knew Aramaic and Greek
- Left his toll booth, after Jesus came and said, "Follow Me."
- Held a great banquet for Jesus and invited all his tax collector friends

STORY IN BIBLE Genesis 14; Psalm 110; Hebrews 7

BORN Around 2100 BC

NAME MEANING "My King Is Righteous"

OCCUPATION Priest of God

CONTEMPORARY Abraham

CLAIM TO FAME Blessed Abraham

- Called the King of Salem, a Canaanite city that would become Jerusalem

- Also known as King of Righteousness and King of Peace (Shalom)

- His story is found in just four verses of the Old Testament

- Was a priest chosen by Yahweh before the time of the Levites

- Greeted Abraham who had just won a battle against the Canaanites. Gave him bread and wine and blessed him.

- Was given a tenth of Abraham's goods

- Compared to Jesus in Hebrews 7, where it says he had no beginning and no end, no mother or father, indicating he was like a heavenly being

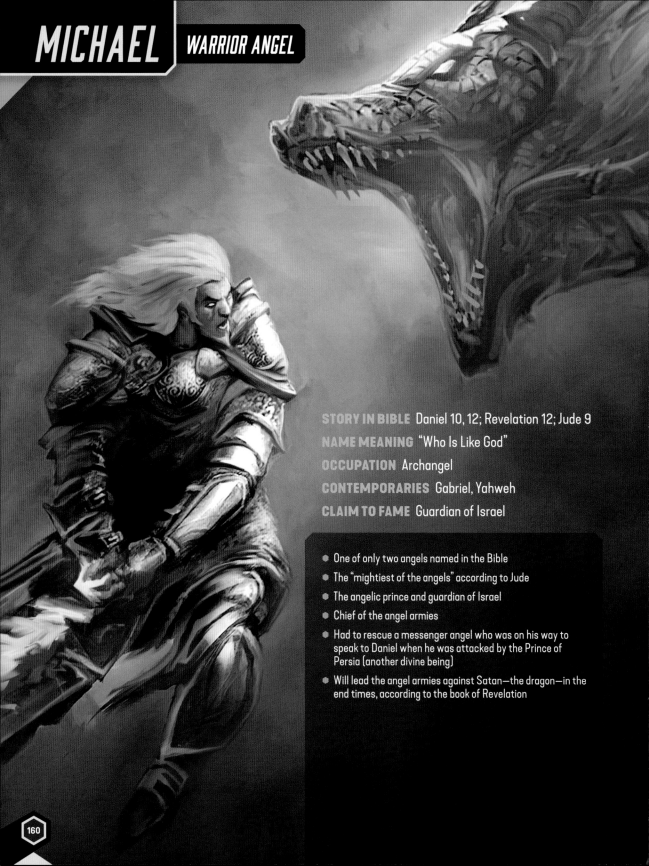

MICHAEL | WARRIOR ANGEL

STORY IN BIBLE Daniel 10, 12; Revelation 12; Jude 9

NAME MEANING "Who Is Like God"

OCCUPATION Archangel

CONTEMPORARIES Gabriel, Yahweh

CLAIM TO FAME Guardian of Israel

- One of only two angels named in the Bible
- The "mightiest of the angels" according to Jude
- The angelic prince and guardian of Israel
- Chief of the angel armies
- Had to rescue a messenger angel who was on his way to speak to Daniel when he was attacked by the Prince of Persia (another divine being)
- Will lead the angel armies against Satan—the dragon—in the end times, according to the book of Revelation

STORY IN BIBLE Exodus 2, 15; Numbers 12, 20

BORN 1500s BC in Egypt

NAME MEANING "Strong-Willed"

OCCUPATION Prophetess

RELATIVES Brothers—Moses, Aaron. Mother—Jochebed. Father—Amram.

CLAIM TO FAME Watched over her baby brother Moses; helped lead the Israelites in the wilderness

- Saw Pharaoh's daughter pick up baby Moses out of the river and suggested her mother as a nurse
- Led the women in a song of victory and praise after the crossing of the Red Sea
- Was known for her singing and dancing
- Called a prophetess
- Once opposed Moses' leadership and was stricken with leprosy
- Died in the wilderness at Kadesh

MORDECAI   HERO OF THE JEWS

STORY IN BIBLE Book of Esther

BORN 540 BC in Persia

NAME MEANING "Little Man"

OCCUPATION Court official, later prime minister of Susa

RELATIVES Cousin—Esther (Hadassah). Father—Jair.

CONTEMPORARIES Haman, Xerxes

CLAIM TO FAME Helped to save the Jewish race from a holocaust

- Guardian of Queen Esther
- Official of the Persian city of Susa
- Sat at king's gate and watched people coming and going
- Once prevented an assassination of the Persian king
- Helped Esther thwart a plot to annihilate the Jews in Persia
- Honored by the king and given job of prime minister

STORY IN BIBLE 2 Kings 5; Luke 4

BORN 850 BC in Syria

NAME MEANING "Pleasant"

OCCUPATION Military commander

CONTEMPORARIES Elisha, Ben-Hadad II, King of Syria

CLAIM TO FAME A Gentile healed by the God of Israel

Naaman was a successful and famous Syrian general who was afflicted with a terrible skin disease known as leprosy. He had a Jewish slave girl who told him to go to Elisha the prophet in Israel for healing. So Naaman went, taking loads of money with him. But Elisha never even came out to see him personally, just told him to go and wash in the Jordan seven times. Naaman was insulted by Elisha's snub, but he followed the instructions anyway and was miraculously healed. He became a follower of the Lord and asked to bring some soil from Israel back to his homeland, so he could continue to worship the Lord on holy ground even while serving his pagan king.

Jesus cited Naaman as the only leper to be healed by the Lord in Elisha's time—and he wasn't even a Jew. The people were so angry when Jesus said this that they tried to throw him off a cliff.

MOSES | *PRINCE OF EGYPT*

STORY IN BIBLE Exodus through Deuteronomy

BORN Around 1526 BC in Egypt

NAME MEANING "To Draw Out" (Hebrew) or "Born" (Egyptian)

OCCUPATION Prince, shepherd, leader of Israelites

RELATIVES Father—Amran. Mother—Jochebed. Brother—Aaron. Sister—Miriam. Wife—Zipporah. Father-in-law—Jethro (or Reuel). Sons—Gershom and Eliezer.

CLAIM TO FAME Led the Israelites to the promised land

- Greatest figure of the Old Testament
- Age 80 when God called him to lead the people
- Might have stuttered
- Committed murder
- Wrote songs, including Psalm 90 in the Bible
- Died on a mountain, and God buried him in a hidden place
- 120 years old when he died

STRENGTHS
- Great spiritual leader
- Wilderness training and experience
- The most humble man of his day
- Trusted in God

WEAKNESSES
- Violent temper
- Often tried to do everything himself
- Sometimes unwilling to obey God's commands

Moses was born a Hebrew in Egypt at the time when the pharaoh was having all newborn Hebrew boys killed. Moses' mother placed him in a basket and sent him downriver. Thanks to God's providence, Pharaoh's daughter pulled Moses from the river and raised him as her own.

At the age of forty, Moses was forced to flee the palace after he killed an Egyptian overseer. He lived in exile for forty years as a humble shepherd, probably thinking that would be it for him.

But then the Lord appeared to him in a burning bush and told him he was to lead his people out of Egypt. After several dramatic confrontations with Pharaoh and ten nasty plagues, Moses succeeded. He went from herding sheep to herding a large flock of very ornery people.

It took forty years for the Israelites to reach their destination. Moses himself was not allowed to enter the promised land, but he did get a glimpse of it, right before his death. And he's one of the few people in the Bible who saw God face-to-face and lived to tell about it.

DID YOU KNOW?
A "Moses basket" is often a term used for a small woven baby carrier.

NABOTH

WRONG PLACE, WRONG TIME

Naboth had the bad luck of owning a vineyard right next to King Ahab's palace. When Ahab decided he wanted to buy the vineyard to make it into his vegetable garden, Naboth refused. It was ancestral land and couldn't be sold. That didn't stop Ahab. He complained to his wife Jezebel, who had Naboth and his sons stoned to death. Ahab got Naboth's vineyard. But the prophet Elijah told Ahab that because of this wicked deed, dogs would lick up his blood as they had Naboth's. Not long after, Ahab was killed in battle, and his blood was licked up by dogs. When Ahab's son Joram was killed, his body was thrown onto Naboth's land.

STORY IN BIBLE 1 Kings 21; 2 Kings 9

BORN Around 900 BC in Jezreel

NAME MEANING "Sprout"

OCCUPATION Vineyard owner

RELATIVES Son—Unnamed

CONTEMPORARIES Ahab, Jezebel

CLAIM TO FAME Murdered over a plot of land

STORY IN BIBLE Book of Ruth

BORN Around 1225 BC in Bethlehem

NAME MEANING "Sweet"

OCCUPATION Mother

RELATIVES Husband—Elimelech. Sons—Mahlon and Chilion. Daughters-in Law—Ruth and Orpah.

CLAIM TO FAME Mother-in-law of Ruth

Naomi had moved with her husband from Bethlehem to the pagan land of Moab when there was a famine in Judah. Her sons married Moabite women. But when her husband and both sons died, Naomi was so brokenhearted that she changed her name to Mara, which means bitter.

Poor and destitute, she and her daughters-in-law, Ruth and Orpah, journeyed back toward Judah, where Naomi still had relatives. Orpah turned back halfway, but Ruth vowed to stay with Naomi, choosing to be a part of Naomi's family and worship her God.

Once back in Judah, Naomi helped Ruth win the favor of her relative Boaz, who fell in love with Ruth, married her, and gave both women a home and family. Naomi, who had once felt cursed by God, now knew she was blessed.

NATHAN

STORY IN BIBLE 2 Samuel 7; 12

BORN Around 1000 BC

NAME MEANING "He Gave"

OCCUPATION Prophet

RELATIVES Sons—Zabad, Azariah

CONTEMPORARIES David, Solomon

CLAIM TO FAME Rebuked David for his sin

- Advisor and prophet for King David and King Solomon
- Told David the Lord did not want him to build the temple.
- Used a parable (a made-up story) about a rich man and a baby lamb to rebuke David for his sin with Bathsheba
- Wrote histories of David and Solomon
- In charge of Solomon's education
- Helped to make sure Solomon was named David's successor and anointed Solomon king
- His sons were high officials in the court

NATHANAEL

STORY IN BIBLE John 1

BORN First century AD

NAME MEANING "Gift of God"

OCCUPATION Apostle

CONTEMPORARIES
Jesus, Philip, the disciples

CLAIM TO FAME
One of Jesus' twelve apostles

- From Cana in Galilee
- Also called Bartholomew, meaning "son of plowman." (The apostle Matthew also had a second name: Levi).
- Best friends with the apostle Philip
- Well-versed in the Scriptures
- Initially didn't believe in Jesus because He was from Nazareth
- Was so amazed when Jesus said He had seen him "under a fig tree" that he declared Jesus to be the Son of God and King of Israel. (Being under a fig tree often referred to someone reading or studying.)
- Was with the disciples who saw the risen Jesus on the shore of the Sea of Galilee

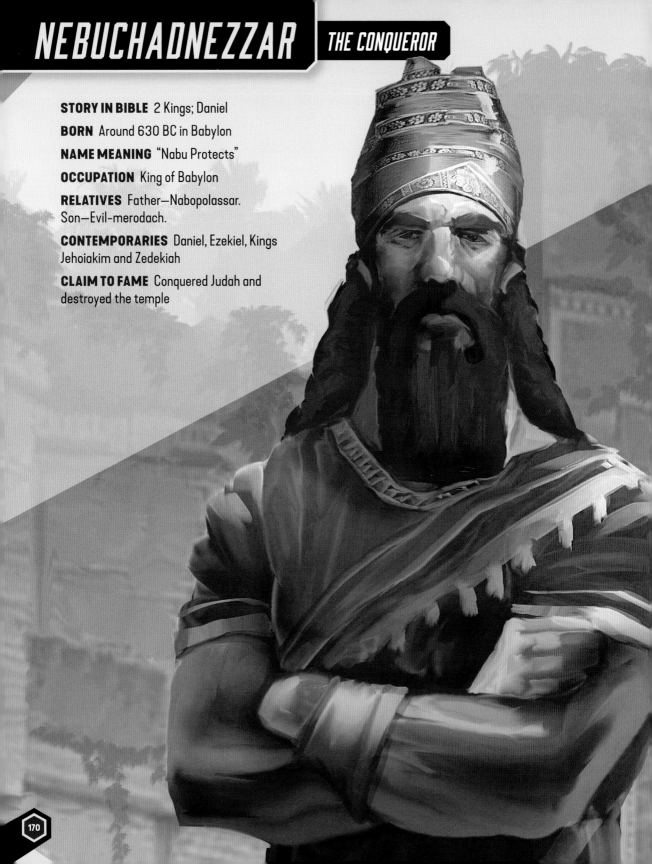

NEBUCHADNEZZAR THE CONQUEROR

STORY IN BIBLE 2 Kings; Daniel

BORN Around 630 BC in Babylon

NAME MEANING "Nabu Protects"

OCCUPATION King of Babylon

RELATIVES Father—Nabopolassar. Son—Evil-merodach.

CONTEMPORARIES Daniel, Ezekiel, Kings Jehoiakim and Zedekiah

CLAIM TO FAME Conquered Judah and destroyed the temple

The great conqueror Nebuchadnezzar had a scary dream about a huge statue. He asked his court magicians not only to interpret his dream but first to tell him what it was—they couldn't do it. The king was so mad he demanded they all be killed. But Daniel, one of the exiles from Israel, intervened. He prayed all night, and the Lord revealed to him not only what the dream was but what it meant. Nebuchadnezzar was so impressed with Daniel's ability to explain his dream that he declared Daniel's God must be the greatest of all gods, and he gave Daniel the job of chief of all his court officials.

Although Nebuchadnezzar never followed the God of Israel, he seemed to recognize God's power and might through the works of Daniel. Little did Nebuchadnezzar know that he was being used by God to discipline His people and bring them back to Him.

DID YOU KNOW?

Nebuchadnezzar built the "Hanging Gardens of Babylon," one of the Seven Wonders of the World.

- Second and most powerful king of Babylon
- Named after Nebo, Babylonian god of wisdom and agriculture
- Destroyed Jerusalem and the temple, wiping out the Jewish nation
- Had King Zedekiah's eyes put out and killed his sons
- Carried much of the population of Judah into exile
- Brought Ezekiel, Daniel, and Daniel's three friends to Babylon
- Built many cities, palaces, and temples
- Went mad for a while and lived like an animal but then recovered

STRENGTHS
- Great military leader
- Recognized the abilities of his Jewish captives
- Allowed Daniel to worship his God

WEAKNESSES
- Excessively proud and arrogant
- Very violent
- Did not heed the Lord's warnings

NEHEMIAH

THE WALL BUILDER

STORY IN BIBLE Book of Nehemiah

BORN Around 500 BC in Persia

NAME MEANING "The Lord Comforts"

OCCUPATION Cupbearer/governor

RELATIVES Father—Hachaliah

CONTEMPORARIES King Artaxerxes I, Esther, Ezra, Malachi

CLAIM TO FAME Rebuilt the wall of Jerusalem

DID YOU KNOW?

Nehemiah rebuilt Jerusalem's wall in only fifty-two days.

- Jewish exile living in Persia
- Cupbearer to King Artaxerxes
- Organized the rebuilding of the wall of Jerusalem
- Became governor of Judah

STRENGTHS
- Courageous
- Great planner and organizer
- Great moral leader
- Prayerful and compassionate

Nehemiah's first job was to taste the king's wine to make sure it wasn't poisoned. So he had to be a pretty brave guy. When he heard of the deplorable conditions in Jerusalem, he asked the king to allow him to return there to fix the situation. Artaxerxes agreed and made Nehemiah the governor of Judah.

Nehemiah arrived in Jerusalem to find the walls around the city destroyed. He got right to work, organizing the people to rebuild the walls and institute proper worship of the Lord. Local leaders tried to stop Nehemiah's work—he had to station guards with weapons right next to the builders to protect them. Despite many setbacks, the wall was completed in record time. Unfortunately, after he returned to Persia twelve years later, the Israelites fell into worshiping idols again.

NICODEMUS

JESUS' SECRET FOLLOWER

- Pharisee, teacher of the law, and member of Sanhedrin
- Visited Jesus at night in secret to learn more about Him
- Was the first to hear Jesus speak the words of John 3:16: "For God loved the world in this way: He gave his only Son, so that everyone who believes in him will not perish but have eternal life."
- Was told by Jesus he needed to be "born again"
- Defended Jesus when the Pharisees wanted to arrest Him
- Risked his reputation when he helped Joseph of Arimathea bury Jesus

STORY IN BIBLE John 3; 7; 19

BORN Around 25 BC

NAME MEANING "Innocent of Blood"

OCCUPATION Pharisee

CONTEMPORARIES Jesus, Pilate, Joseph of Arimathea

CLAIM TO FAME Jewish leader who believed in Jesus

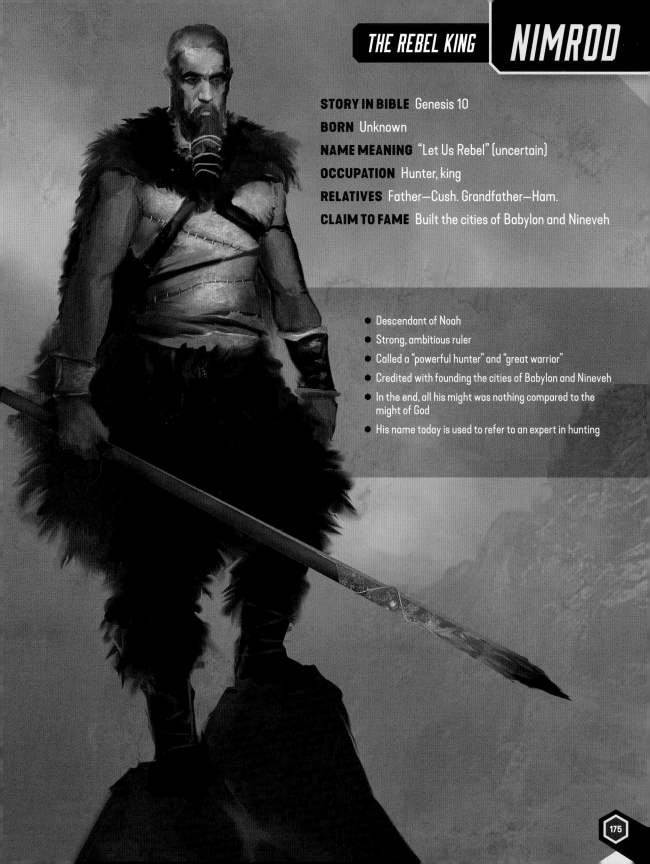

THE REBEL KING NIMROD

STORY IN BIBLE Genesis 10

BORN Unknown

NAME MEANING "Let Us Rebel" (uncertain)

OCCUPATION Hunter, king

RELATIVES Father—Cush. Grandfather—Ham.

CLAIM TO FAME Built the cities of Babylon and Nineveh

- Descendant of Noah
- Strong, ambitious ruler
- Called a "powerful hunter" and "great warrior"
- Credited with founding the cities of Babylon and Nineveh
- In the end, all his might was nothing compared to the might of God
- His name today is used to refer to an expert in hunting

NOAH
THE LAST GOOD GUY

STORY IN BIBLE Genesis 5–10

BORN Unknown

NAME MEANING "To Rest"

OCCUPATION Shipbuilder, zookeeper, farmer

RELATIVES Father—Lamech. Grandfather—Methuselah. Sons—Shem, Ham, Japheth.

CLAIM TO FAME Built an ark and survived a worldwide flood

DID YOU KNOW?
Noah's ark was one and a half football fields long (but only half the length of the Titanic).

By the time of Noah, people had become so wicked that God decided to give humanity a do-over. So He told Noah, the only righteous man left on earth, to build a really big boat. On dry land.

Noah was five hundred years old when he started building the ark. The work took him one hundred years. Then the Lord filled the boat with every species of animal. Noah, his wife, his three sons and their wives all boarded the ark when the rain started and the water came up from under the earth. It rained for forty days straight. Everything in the whole world was destroyed. But Noah and his family were saved.

The ark floated freely for one hundred fifty days before the waters receded. It came to rest on the mountains of Ararat. God placed a rainbow in the sky as a promise that He would never again destroy the world with a flood. Then Noah and his family left the ark and established a new dynasty on the earth, possibly with a whole bunch of pets.

- Lived ten generations after Adam
- A descendent of Adam's son Seth
- Was first person God allowed to kill animals for food
- Died at the age of 950, 350 years after the Flood

STRENGTHS
- Righteous man who walked faithfully with God
- Obedient to God's instructions
- Restarted the human race
- Excellent boat builder

WEAKNESSES
- Drunkenness
- Lack of discipline over his sons

OG

KING OF GIANTS

STORY IN BIBLE Deuteronomy 3; Numbers 21

BORN Around 1500 BC

NAME MEANING "Long-necked"

OCCUPATION King of Bashan

RELATIVES Four sons (unnamed)

CONTEMPORARY Moses

CLAIM TO FAME Giant king defeated by Moses

- King of Bashan
- Was a Rephaim, one of the giants descended from the Nephilim
- Greatly feared by the Israelites, and one of the reasons they didn't want to go into Canaan in the first place
- His kingdom, Bashan, contained sixty walled cities
- His bed was more than thirteen feet long
- Killed by Moses and the Israelite army due to God's provision
- Sons also killed, thereby destroying the Rephaim in Canaan
- His kingdom was given to the half tribe of Manasseh

STORY IN BIBLE Acts 6; 8; 21

BORN First century AD

NAME MEANING "Friend of Horses"

OCCUPATION Evangelist, deacon

RELATIVES Four daughters (unnamed)

CONTEMPORARIES Paul, Stephen, disciples

CLAIM TO FAME Preached to an Ethiopian court official

Philip the Evangelist is often confused with the Philip who was one of the original twelve apostles. But this Philip was the first traveling missionary. He went to preach to the Samaritans, whom most Jews avoided. Many people were healed and delivered from demons by his work, which was so amazing that one sorcerer named Simon wanted to buy the power of the Holy Spirit.

One day an angel led Philip into a desert place in the south, where he came upon a court official from Ethiopia sitting in a chariot, reading the Scriptures. Philip offered to explain to the man what he was reading and then led him to be baptized. Right after that, the Holy Spirit literally whisked Philip away to another place. But the Ethiopian went back home rejoicing, for he had found Jesus.

PAUL | APOSTLE TO THE GENTILES

STORY IN BIBLE Acts and Letters of Paul

BORN Around 4 BC in Tarsus

NAME MEANING "Little"

OCCUPATION Pharisee, missionary

RELATIVES Sister and nephew (unnamed)

CONTEMPORARIES Peter, the disciples, Gamaliel, Luke, Barnabas, Timothy, Silas, Emperor Nero

CLAIM TO FAME Wrote nearly half the books of the New Testament

Paul was on his way to Damascus with letters to arrest Christians when he was stopped in his tracks by a radiant light and the voice of Jesus calling to him. Paul was blinded for three days, until a Christian named Ananias laid hands on him and restored his sight. He knew then that Jesus was truly the Son of God. Although Paul had been a ruthless persecutor of Christians, he changed and spent the rest of his life proclaiming Jesus' name all over the known world.

Before this event, Paul (known as Saul) had been a well-respected Pharisee living a comfortable and safe life. Afterward, his life became quite dangerous. He was mocked, beaten, flogged, imprisoned, stoned, and run out of town for his preaching. He embarked on three separate missionary journeys, traveling over ten thousand miles on foot, enduring shipwrecks, hunger, sleeplessness, persecution, threats on his life, discouragement, and loneliness to tell people about Jesus. When he was arrested, he spent his time in jail writing letters to encourage and correct the churches he had founded; those letters became a large part of the New Testament. Paul allowed nothing to keep him from preaching of the love and salvation of Jesus Christ to the world.

- Hebrew name was Saul ("asked for")
- Jewish Pharisee educated by the famous teacher Gamaliel
- From tribe of Benjamin
- Born in a Gentile city with Roman citizenship
- Founded several Christian churches in Asia Minor
- Believed to have been executed in Rome by Emperor Nero

STRENGTHS
- Educated, accomplished writer
- Bold speaker
- Tireless in bringing the gospel to all the corners of the world
- Obedient to God's calling

WEAKNESSES
- Initially opposed Christianity and persecuted Christians
- Oversaw the stoning of Stephen
- Had an undisclosed, chronic physical limitation

PETER | THE ROCK

STORY IN BIBLE Matthew; Mark; Luke; John; Acts of the Apostles; 1 and 2 Peter

BORN Around 10 BC in Bethsaida

NAME MEANING "Rock"

OCCUPATION Fisherman

RELATIVES Father—Jonas. Brother—Andrew.

CONTEMPORARIES Jesus, the disciples, Paul

CLAIM TO FAME Jesus' apostle and leader of the first Christians

Once Peter spent all night fishing but caught nothing. In the morning, Jesus appeared and told him to let down his net one more time. Although Peter had given up hope, he obeyed, and he caught so many fish that the net started to break.

Such was Peter's life with Jesus. Miracle upon miracle. Although he was courageous and devoted to Jesus, he often said and did things without thinking them through, getting himself into trouble.

Just like us.

There was the time he walked on water but then got scared and started to sink. Or the time Jesus rebuked him for cutting off the ear of one of the soldiers who had come to arrest Jesus in the Garden of Gethsemane. And then there was the time Peter denied even knowing Jesus at all.

Yet nothing Peter did would stop God from using him for His purpose. Just like us.

- Fisherman
- Lived in Capernaum with wife and mother-in-law
- Introduced to Jesus by his brother Andrew
- Original name was Simon ("he has heard")
- Walked on water with Jesus
- Witnessed the Transfiguration
- Key leader of "The Way" after Jesus' ascension to heaven

STRENGTHS

- Loyal follower of Jesus
- Became leader of the apostles
- Powerful preacher

WEAKNESSES

- Impulsive and brash
- Denied Jesus three times
- Initially prejudiced against Gentiles

DID YOU KNOW?

Peter was probably the only apostle over age thirty, because only he and Jesus were required to pay the temple tax (Jesus got the money from the mouth of a fish).

PHARAOH | *KING OF THE EXODUS*

STORY IN BIBLE Exodus

BORN Around 1500 BC

NAME MEANING "Great House"

OCCUPATION Ruler of Egypt

CONTEMPORARIES Moses, Aaron

CLAIM TO FAME Let the Jewish slaves go free—sort of

- King of Egypt
- Pharaohs were considered representatives of gods.
- The word *pharaoh* refers not only to the king but also to the palace in which he lived.
- Twelve pharaohs are mentioned in the Bible, most not named.

STRENGTHS
- Strong leader
- Built many great monuments and buildings

WEAKNESS
- Stubborn and hard-hearted
- Vengeful and cruel

When this particular unnamed pharaoh took over the rule of Egypt, the Israelites had been enslaved for some time. This pharaoh forced the Israelites to make bricks out of mud for one of his massive building projects. When Moses—whom this pharaoh did not know—returned to Egypt to confront him about letting the Jewish people go free to worship in the desert, he stubbornly refused. He liked having slaves do all the work.

God sent plagues to convince Pharaoh to free the Israelites. But even after enduring nine horrific plagues, Pharaoh wouldn't budge. For the tenth plague, God told the Israelites to paint their door frames in lamb's blood, for He was going to pass over the nation and cause the death of every first-born son in any household that had no blood on its door. Pharaoh's own son was one of those who died.

Finally, Pharaoh let the Jewish people go free. But then he changed his mind and chased after them with an army, cornering them at the Red Sea. God parted the sea, allowing the Israelites to cross on dry land. When Pharaoh's army tried to follow, the sea came in and swallowed them up.

DID YOU KNOW?

The pharaohs wore a crown that had an image of the cobra goddess, which they thought would protect them by spitting flames at their enemies.

PHILIP

A BRAINY APOSTLE

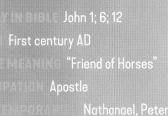

STORY IN BIBLE John 1; 6; 12

BORN First century AD

NAME MEANING "Friend of Horses"

OCCUPATION Apostle

CONTEMPORARIES Nathanael, Peter, Andrew, Jesus, the disciples

CLAIM TO FAME One of the twelve apostles

- From Bethsaida in Galilee
- A follower of John the Baptist
- Was the fifth apostle to follow Jesus
- Introduced his friend Nathanael to Jesus
- Probably educated and spoke Greek (his name was Greek)
- Had connections to the Greeks living in Judea
- One of the first to proclaim Jesus as the Messiah
- Knew the Hebrew Scriptures very well
- Put to the test when Jesus asked him to get food for a big crowd
- According to tradition, preached in Greece, Syria, and western Turkey

PHINEHAS

STORY IN BIBLE Numbers 25

BORN 1400s BC

NAME MEANING "Dark-skinned"

OCCUPATION Priest

RELATIVES Father—Eleazar. Grandfathers—Aaron, Jethro. Son—Abishua.

CONTEMPORARY Moses

CLAIM TO FAME Stopped a plague sent by God

Phinehas was in charge of the gatekeepers of the tabernacle, also called the tent of meeting, during the time of the exodus. When the Israelites got involved with a nearby tribe of Midianites and began worshiping pagan gods, God became angry. He demanded all idolaters be killed and struck the camp with plague. Phinehas, enraged by the way his people were acting, took up a spear and killed an Israelite tribal leader as well as the Midianite woman he was with. This act stopped the plague and saved the lives of everyone in the camp. In the ensuing battle against the Midianites, Phinehas the priest of Aaron led twelve thousand men to victory and was greatly honored by the Lord.

PONTIUS PILATE | *AN IMPERFECT PREFECT*

STORY IN BIBLE Matthew 27; Mark 15; Luke 23; John 18–19

BORN Around 20 BC

NAME MEANING "Armed with a Spear"

OCCUPATION Roman governor (prefect) of Judea

CONTEMPORARIES Jesus, Tiberius Caesar, Annas, Caiaphas, Herod Antipas

CLAIM TO FAME Condemned Jesus to death

- Roman governor of Judea at the time of Jesus' arrest
- Appointed by Tiberius Caesar
- Lived in Caesarea, only went to Jerusalem for special occasions

STRENGTHS
- Strove to keep peace
- Tried to set Jesus free

WEAKNESSES
- Often cruel
- Gave into the Jewish leaders out of fear

Pilate's hatred of the Jews was well known. He'd even killed Jews and mixed their blood with the animal sacrifices to Roman gods. But he knew Jesus was innocent, and something must have told him that killing Jesus was a bad idea. Even his wife told him not to do it, for she'd had a dream about Jesus that frightened her.

Pilate tried to get Herod to condemn Jesus. Herod refused. Then Pilate offered to release Jesus in celebration of the Passover. But the crowd chose the criminal Barabbas instead. Pilate had Jesus flogged, hoping that would satisfy the mob. It didn't. He begged Jesus to declare His innocence. Jesus was silent.

In the end Pilate succumbed to the pressure, afraid of losing his job or his life. As it turned out, he did lose his job just a few years later. And some say he even took his own life. Did he feel guilty for what he'd done? Although he had killed Jews in the past with no hesitation whatsoever, something about Jesus had made Pilate very afraid.

DID YOU KNOW?
The "Pilate Stone," a block of stone inscribed with Pilate's name, was found by archaeologists in a theatre building in Caesarea. It proved that Pontius Pilate did exist and was governor of Judea during the time of Jesus.

PRISCILLA AND AQUILA

CORINTH'S POWER COUPLE

STORY IN BIBLE Acts 18

BORN First century AD

NAME MEANING Priscilla—"Venerable." Aquila—"Eagle." (both uncertain)

OCCUPATION Tentmakers or leather-workers

CONTEMPORARIES Paul, Apollos

CLAIM TO FAME Helped Paul to found the churches in Corinth and Ephesus

- Early Jewish Christians
- Had been exiled from Rome when Jews were forced out by Emperor Claudius
- Set up churches in their own home in Corinth and Ephesus
- Paul lived with them for a time, making tents and preaching with them
- Risked their lives to help Paul
- Accompanied Paul to Ephesus
- Taught the accurate gospel to Apollos
- Returned to Rome to preach to the Christians there for a time
- In his last letter, Paul gave his final greetings to Priscilla and Aquila

QUEEN OF SHEBA

STORY IN BIBLE 1 Kings 10; 2 Chronicles 9

BORN Around 1000 BC

NAME MEANING Real name unknown

OCCUPATION Queen

RELATIVES Unknown

CONTEMPORARY Solomon

CLAIM TO FAME Traveled far to visit King Solomon

- From Sheba (or Saba), which could have been in southern Arabia or Ethiopia
- Of unknown ancestry
- Heard of the wisdom of Solomon and came personally to see for herself
- Tested Solomon with difficult questions and was impressed with his answers
- Was astounded by the splendor of Solomon's palace
- Praised the God of Israel for putting Solomon on the throne
- She gave Solomon a huge amount of gold, jewels, and frankincense. Frankincense was a resin from the Boswellia tree in southern Arabia and Ethiopia and was the most valuable commodity at the time.

RACHEL PRETTY WOMAN

STORY IN BIBLE Genesis 29–35

BORN 1900s BC

NAME MEANING "Ewe"

OCCUPATION Shepherdess

RELATIVES Husband—Jacob. Aunt—Rebekah. Father—Laban. Sister—Leah.

CLAIM TO FAME Mother of Joseph and Benjamin

- Lived in Haran (northern Syria)
- Beautiful youngest daughter of Laban
- Married Jacob (so did her sister Leah)
- Jacob had to work for fourteen years to marry her.
- Unable to bear children at first
- Tended to be willful and scheming
- Stole her father's household gods ("teraphim") before leaving home, perhaps believing they would bring good luck
- Died while giving birth to Benjamin on the road to Bethlehem

SCRIPTURE REFERENCE Genesis 24–27

BIRTH Around 2000s BC

NAME MEANING "Finest Calf"

OCCUPATION Mother and wife

RELATIVES Husband—Isaac. Father—Bethuel. Great-uncle and Father-in-Law—Abraham. Brother—Laban. Sons—Jacob, Esau.

CLAIM TO FAME Helped Jacob steal his brother's blessing

- Lived in Paddan-aram (northwest Mesopotamia)
- Very beautiful
- Married her second cousin Isaac in one of the sweetest love stories of the Bible
- Unable to bear children for twenty years before finally giving birth to twins, Jacob and Esau
- God promised her that her older son (Esau) would serve the younger
- Tricked Isaac into giving his blessing to Jacob by having Jacob pretend to be Esau
- Had Jacob sent to her brother Laban when she learned that Esau was planning to kill him
- Died before Jacob returned

RAHAB | FROM HARLOT TO HEROINE

Joshua 2; 6

Around 1430 BC

"Pride"

Innkeeper and prostitute

Husband—Salmon. Son—Boaz.

Joshua

Heroine of the battle of Jericho

- Resident of Jericho
- Listed in the Hall of Faith in Hebrews
- Ancestor of David
- Listed in the genealogy of Jesus

STRENGTHS

- Kind, compassionate, and merciful
- Showed great courage and cleverness in hiding the spies from the soldiers

WEAKNESSES

- Was a pagan and a prostitute, but later married an Israelite and accepted the Lord as her God

It's a story worthy of a movie plot: Rahab, a fallen woman living in a fallen city, is visited by two men from Israel's camp. They've come to scout out the city before the Israelites attack. Although she is a Canaanite woman, Rahab gives the men shelter in her home, which is built into the city wall. When soldiers come looking for the men, she hides them under bundles of flax drying on her roof until the soldiers leave. Then she helps them escape by lowering them from her window with a rope. The spies tell her that if she ties a scarlet cord to her window, she and her family would be spared when Jericho was destroyed. And that is exactly what happened.

Rahab later married a prince of the tribe of Judah named Salmon. We don't know if she lived happily ever after, but her bravery and shrewdness forever marked her as a hero.

REHOBOAM — AN ARROGANT KING

STORY IN BIBLE
1 Kings 11–14; 2 Chronicles 11–12

BORN Around 975 BC

NAME MEANING "He Enlarges the People"

OCCUPATION King of Judah

RELATIVES Father—Solomon.
Mother—Naamah. Son—Abijah.

CONTEMPORARIES Jeroboam (king of northern kingdom of Israel), Shishak (king of Egypt)

CLAIM TO FAME His rule led to the splitting of the kingdom

- Son and successor of King Solomon
- Mother was an Ammonite (a pagan)
- Took advice from the wrong people
- Refused to lighten the heavy labor loads imposed by his father
- Caused a rebellion that split the kingdom
- Became the king of Judah, one of only two tribes that remained loyal to him
- Led the people to idolatry
- Had to surrender much of the palace and temple treasure to the Egyptians when they invaded Jerusalem
- Like Solomon, took many foreign women as wives
- Had twenty-eight sons and sixty daughters

SAMARITAN WOMAN

STORY IN BIBLE John 4

BORN First century AD

NAME MEANING Unknown

OCCUPATION Unknown

RELATIVES Unknown

CONTEMPORARY Jesus

CLAIM TO FAME Met Jesus at a well

We don't know her name, but her encounter with Jesus has resounded through the centuries.

Jesus was lingering near Jacob's well in Samaria when a woman came to draw water. Jesus asked her for a drink. She was shocked, for Jews never associated with Samaritans. Still, she engaged in a conversation with Jesus, and she discovered that He knew all about her life, including all the sins she had committed. But He also revealed to her His true identity—that of the Messiah. The woman left her water jar and went back to town, proclaiming that she had met the Christ. The townsfolk made their way to the well to see for themselves, and they too believed.

Who was this woman? We will never know in this life. She was not considered a good woman even in her own village, and yet Jesus chose to reveal His identity to her and to give her a gift no one else can give: living water, which meant the Holy Spirit.

RUTH

A WOMAN REDEEMED

STORY IN BIBLE Book of Ruth

BORN Around 1175 BC

NAME MEANING "Refreshed"

OCCUPATION Grain-gatherer

RELATIVES First husband—Chilion. Second husband—Boaz. Mother-in-law—Naomi. Son—Obed.

CONTEMPORARY Gideon

CLAIM TO FAME Left her homeland to be with Naomi

DID YOU KNOW?

Although not Jewish, Ruth is named in Matthew's genealogy of Jesus.

Ruth, a Moabite woman, married a Jewish man whose family had moved to Moab to escape a famine in Judah. When the man and his brother and father died, Ruth and her sister-in-law, Orpah, were left with their mother-in-law, Naomi. Naomi began the journey back to Bethlehem, her hometown. Although Orpah turned back, Ruth stayed with Naomi. She had decided she would make Israel her home and Naomi's God her God.

Things were tough for Ruth and Naomi at first. They were very poor. Ruth went out every day to pick up bits of grain from the farms nearby. Soon she was noticed by a kind land-owner named Boaz, who turned out to be a relative of Naomi's and therefore able to help women in their predicament. Thanks to some maneuvering on Naomi's part, Boaz ended up falling in love with Ruth. They got married and had a son, Obed, who was the father of Jesse, the father of David, the future king.

The fact that Ruth is named in the lineage of Jesus demonstrates how God would include people of all nations, not just the Jews, in His plan for saving the world from sin and death.

- From Moab
- Moabites were pagans who practiced child sacrifice
- Young widow

STRENGTHS
- Loyal, compassionate
- Brave, willing to venture into a new land
- Devout, believing in the Lord

SAMSON

SUPER MAN

STORY IN BIBLE Judges 13–16

BORN Around 1100 BC in Zorah in Canaan

NAME MEANING "Child of the Sun"

OCCUPATION Judge, deliverer

RELATIVES Father—Manoah. Wife—Unnamed (Philistine).

CONTEMPORARY Delilah

CLAIM TO FAME Started a Hebrew revolt against Philistine rule

The birth of Samson, like Jesus, was announced to his parents by an angel.

- Was a Nazirite, which meant he should never drink wine, eat anything unclean, touch a dead body, or cut his hair
- From the tribe of Dan
- Led Israel as a judge for twenty years
- Killed a lion on the way to propose to his wife
- Once fastened torches to three hundred foxes and sent them into Philistine territory to burn their grain fields
- Used the jawbone of a donkey to kill one thousand Philistines
- Loved to tell riddles
- Removed the gates of the city of Gaza and carried them forty-five miles to Hebron
- Mentioned in the Hall of Faith in Hebrews

STRENGTHS

- Extreme physical strength
- Very intelligent
- Dedicated to God before he was born
- Helped to free the Israelites from Philistine oppression

WEAKNESSES

- Broke his vows frequently
- Violent temper
- Trusted the wrong people
- Used his gifts unwisely

Samson is the closest thing the Bible gets to a superhero (other than Jesus, of course). He was born with super strength but not with super good judgment. He broke his Nazirite vows. He married a Philistine woman. He made rash bets. He went on murderous rampages, killing more than four thousand men in a private war.

Worst of all, Samson fell in love with a beautiful but treacherous woman named Delilah. The Philistines challenged her to uncover the source of Samson's strength so they could kill him. Delilah asked him for his secret four times before Samson finally told her the truth: if his hair were cut, he would lose all his strength.

You can guess what Delilah did next. As soon as he was asleep, she had Samson's head shaved. The soldiers came. They seized Samson, gouged out his eyes, and led him to prison. Mocked and beaten, he was paraded in front of thousands of Philistines and tied between two pillars in the temple to their god Dagon.

And finally, Samson prayed. He prayed to have his strength back one more time. God answered that prayer. Samson pushed against the two pillars, and they gave way. The entire temple collapsed, killing everyone inside and starting a revolt against the Philistines that would be completed by King David fifty years later.

With this act of supreme sacrifice, Samson at last became the hero God intended him to be. It was a foreshadowing of what would happen 1100 years later, when Jesus, nailed to a cross, would give up His life to save His people from their sins.

STORY IN BIBLE 1 Samuel

BORN Around 1100 BC

NAME MEANING "His Name Is God"

OCCUPATION Prophet

RELATIVES Father—Elkanah. Mother—Hannah.

CONTEMPORARIES Eli, Saul, David

CLAIM TO FAME Anointed the first two kings of Israel

Samuel was the last judge of Israel, for the people had decided they wanted a king. So God directed Samuel to anoint a donkey herder named Saul as king. Saul started out well, but his reign ended in disaster. Samuel constantly rebuked Saul for taking matters into his own hands and refusing to follow God's instructions. But God had already chosen Saul's replacement. God sent Samuel to Bethlehem to anoint the youngest son of Jesse—David—as king.

Samuel died before David became king. But then King Saul, desperate to know the outcome of a battle, hired a medium from En-dor to summon Samuel from the grave (despite the fact that Saul himself had outlawed using mediums to contact the dead). Samuel's ghost appeared to the medium, much to her horror, and rebuked Saul for disturbing him. He also told Saul he would lose the battle and that Saul and his sons would die.

Saul and his sons died in battle the very next day.

- Dedicated to God by his mother before he was born
- Raised in the tabernacle by the high priest Eli
- Anointed Saul and David as kings of Israel
- His prayers gave Israelites victory over the Philistines when God sent a thunderstorm to scatter the enemy
- Traveled around Israel preaching and ministering
- Warned Israel against having a king rule over them

STRENGTHS
- Wise and devout
- Close relationship with God
- Heard God's voice at an early age

WEAKNESSES
- Allowed his own sons to take bribes and abuse their power

SARAH | WORLD'S OLDEST MOTHER

STORY IN BIBLE Genesis 17–25

BORN 2100s BC

NAME MEANING "Princess"

OCCUPATION Wife, mother

RELATIVES Father—Terah. Husband—Abraham.
Half brothers—Abraham, Nahor, Haran. Nephew—Lot. Son—Isaac.

CLAIM TO FAME Had a baby when she was 90

DID YOU KNOW?
Sarah's husband, Abraham, was also her half brother
(they shared the same father).

- From Ur (modern-day Iraq)
- Unable to bear children until God's intervention
- Died at age 127

STRENGTHS

- Brave—endured lots of long-distance moves and even exile
- Very beautiful

WEAKNESSES

- Treated her servants badly
- Her schemes to give Abraham a child caused much anguish in the family
- Kicked Hagar and Ishmael out of the house after Isaac was born

Sarah was the wife of Abraham and the mother of the Jewish nation as we know it. But she is also known as the woman who laughed.

Why did she laugh? Because three men showed up at her husband's tent one day to tell him that Sarah was going to have a baby. She was ninety years old at the time. She had never been able to conceive a child. She thought the three men were probably crazy.

But it turned out that two of the men were angelic beings, and the third was the Lord Himself. And nothing is impossible with the Lord. A year later, Sarah gave birth to a son. And she gave him an appropriate name: Isaac, which means "laughter."

SATAN | *THE BIGGEST LOSER*

STORY IN BIBLE
Genesis 3, the Gospels, Revelation

NAME MEANING
"Accuser, Adversary"

OCCUPATION
Ruler of demonic realm

CLAIM TO FAME
Tempting humans into sin

Other names of Satan: Lucifer, the devil, Beelzebub, Belial, Prince of this world, Prince of the power of the air, the dragon, the old serpent, Tempter, father of lies, Evil one

In the Old Testament, "satan" sometimes refers to a heavenly being who tested or provoked humans to sin.

Satan makes his first appearance in the Bible as a crafty serpent in the garden of Eden, tempting Adam and Eve into disobeying God's command. He is successful, for Eve falls for his ploy and gets Adam to follow suit. They are expelled from the garden forever and cursed. Satan seems to have won.

But God puts a curse on Satan's head as well. And four thousand years later, Jesus shows up to fulfill that curse. Satan tries to tempt Jesus to sin and loses big time. And then with Jesus' resurrection, Satan's hold on humankind is broken. He is defeated, although not yet destroyed.

Satan opposes God, but he isn't the opposite of God. Satan is still under God's power. He can only do what God allows him to do. He shudders and flees at the Name of the Lord.

According to John, the writer of the book of Revelation, Satan's final defeat will come at the end times, when there will be a huge battle with Jesus leading an army of angels against Satan and his demons. Satan, "the great dragon," will be thrown into the lake of fire with all his rebellious angels. And that will be the end of him.

DID YOU KNOW?

The King James Bible uses the name Lucifer to refer to someone who lost great power. This Latin word refers to the planet Venus, and it means "light-bringer."

SAUL | *ISRAEL'S FIRST KING*

STORY IN BIBLE 1 Samuel

BORN Around 1080 BC

NAME MEANING "Asked For"

OCCUPATION Donkey herder, king

RELATIVES Father—Kish. Wives—Ahinoam, Rizpah. Sons—Jonathan, Abinadab, Malchishua, Ish-bosheth. Daughters—Merab, Michal.

CONTEMPORARIES Samuel, David

CLAIM TO FAME First king of Israel

Saul was the most impressive-looking man in Israel. He was like a fairy-tale king—the kind the people had hoped for. He won many battles and was hailed as a hero, along with his son, Jonathan.

But soon Saul started doing things his own way rather than God's way. So God removed his Spirit from Saul and sent an evil spirit to torment him. To soothe this evil spirit, Saul's attendants found a shepherd boy named David to play music on his lyre. Saul didn't know that this was the same boy whom Samuel had already anointed as the next king.

When David killed the Philistine Goliath, the Israelites had found a new hero. Although Saul gave David his daughter Michal in marriage, Saul soon became intent on murdering David, who eventually had to run for his life.

Saul began making rash judgments and poor military decisions. Before his last battle, he was so afraid he hired a medium to raise the ghost of Samuel and ask him what was going to happen. The ghost told him he would die in the battle, along with his sons.

When the battle was all but lost and his sons were dead, Saul—already wounded by an arrow— killed himself so he would not fall into the hands of the Philistines. A sad end to what might have been a promising life.

- Donkey herder
- Tribe of Benjamin
- Went looking for a lost donkey and found Samuel, who anointed him king

STRENGTHS

- Tall, handsome, and humble at first
- Great military leader
- Brave in battle and well-liked by his men

WEAKNESSES

- Impulsive and irrational
- Became prideful and disobedient
- Jealous of David and tried to kill him
- Consulted a medium

DID YOU KNOW?

Saul was so shy that when he was to be presented to the people as king, he hid behind some luggage.

SHADRACH, MESHACH, AND ABEDNEGO

THREE BRAVE FRIENDS

STORY IN BIBLE Daniel 1; 3

BORN Around 620 BC

NAME MEANING Shadrach: "At Command of Aku (moon god)." Meshach: "Who Is What Aku Is." Abednego: "Servant of Nego (wisdom god)."

OCCUPATION Royal advisors to Babylonian king

RELATIVES Unknown

CONTEMPORARIES Daniel, Nebuchadnezzar

CLAIM TO FAME Survived a fiery furnace

- Hebrew names were Hananiah ("the Lord is gracious"), Mishael ("who is like God?"), and Azariah ("the Lord has helped")
- Possibly royal princes from Jerusalem
- Taken to Babylon as hostages a few years before the conquest of Judah
- Good friends of Daniel
- Underwent a three-year instruction to learn Babylonian ways
- Refused to eat food from the royal table

STRENGTHS

- Very intelligent and courageous
- Devoted to the Lord
- Uncompromising in their faith

Although Shadrach, Meshach, and Abednego were hostages from Israel, they excelled in the royal court of Babylon. They were favorites of King Nebuchadnezzar . . . until the day they refused to bow down to a huge golden statue of the king. Furious, Nebuchadnezzar ordered the three friends thrown into a blazing furnace. They told the king that their God could rescue them from the fire, but even if He didn't, they still wouldn't bow down to the statue or any other god.

This made the king even madder. The three friends were tied up and thrown into the fire, which was so hot it killed the executioners. But then to his amazement, Nebuchadnezzar saw four figures "walking around" in the fire, not three—and the fourth one looked like a divine being. He ordered the three friends to come out of the fire, and they did, completely unburnt, not even a tiny bit singed or smelling like smoke. Nebuchadnezzar was so impressed that he praised the God of Israel, who was far greater than any god in Babylon. The king ordered that anyone who insulted God to be torn limb from limb and his house made into a garbage dump.

DID YOU KNOW?

King Nebuchadnezzar's statue was ninety feet tall and nine feet wide.

SILAS | FRIEND TO PETER AND PAUL

STORY IN BIBLE Acts 15–18

BORN First century AD

NAME MEANING "Asked For"

OCCUPATION Missionary

RELATIVES Unknown

CONTEMPORARIES Paul, Peter, Mark, Barnabas, Timothy

CLAIM TO FAME Paul's traveling buddy

- Also known as Silvanus
- Roman citizen living in Jerusalem
- Respected leader in Jerusalem church
- Became Paul's traveling partner after Paul parted ways with Barnabas
- Helped Paul and Peter write some letters

Once Paul and Silas were flogged and thrown into prison in Philippi for exorcizing a demon from a slave girl. Though their feet were bound in stocks so they couldn't move, they sang songs and praised God all night. Suddenly, there was a violent earthquake, and all the doors of the prison flew open. The jailer thought the prisoners had escaped and was about to take his own life for his failure, but Paul and Silas assured him they were still there. The jailer was so amazed that he took Paul and Silas to his own home, washed their wounds, and asked that he and his whole family be baptized.

SIMON MAGUS

STORY IN BIBLE Acts 8

BORN First century AD

NAME MEANING "Simon the Magician"

OCCUPATION Sorcerer

CONTEMPORARIES Peter, John, Philip

CLAIM TO FAME Tried to buy the Holy Spirit's power

Simon Magus was a huge celebrity in his day. The great sorcerer from Samaria so amazed people with his magical powers that they actually called him "The Great Power of God." But then the apostle Philip came to town to preach about Jesus, and Simon, along with many others, believed and was baptized. His faith was only on the surface, however. When Peter and John arrived, Simon offered Peter money so he could have the power of the Holy Spirit that he was witnessing in others: speaking in tongues, healing, performing miracles.

Peter knew then that Simon was not a true believer; all he cared about was power so he could impress people. Peter told Simon his heart was not right and warned him to repent so he would be forgiven. Simon asked Peter to pray for him, but we don't know for sure if Simon was truly repentant. Today the word *simony* refers to using religion for personal profit.

SOLOMON | *A WISE AND FOOLISH KING*

STORY IN BIBLE 2 Samuel; 1 Kings; 1 Chronicles

BORN Around 1000 BC in Jerusalem

NAME MEANING "Peace"

OCCUPATION Third king of Israel

RELATIVES Father—David. Mother—Bathsheba. Son—Rehoboam.

CONTEMPORARIES Nathan the prophet, the Queen of Sheba

CLAIM TO FAME Wisest king in history

- Successor to King David
- Built a spectacular palace
- Built the Temple in Jerusalem according to David's plans
- Greatly increased trade with other nations
- Wrote the Book of Proverbs, the Song of Songs, and the Book of Ecclesiastes

STRENGTHS

- Known for great wisdom
- Extremely wealthy
- Wrote songs and proverbs

WEAKNESSES

- Married pagan women and worshiped their gods
- Proved unfaithful to the Lord
- Levied unfair taxes on the people

When God asked Solomon what he wanted most, Solomon said wisdom so he could rule God's people well. God answered his prayer. Solomon impressed many people with his wisdom, including the Queen of Sheba, who came from far away to test him.

Once two women brought a baby before the king, each claiming to be the mother. To demonstrate who was telling the truth, Solomon ordered the baby to be cut down the middle so each woman would have half. One of the women agreed, but the other woman—the true mother—declared she would rather give up the child than kill him.

Solomon ruled during a long period of peace and prosperity. But as he grew older, he started to make many unwise decisions. He had more than seven hundred wives, many from foreign nations, who led him to worship idols. He imposed heavy taxes on the people to pay for his massive building projects. Soon revolt was in the air.

Solomon was the last king to rule over a united Israel. Because of his disobedience, the Lord declared the nation would be split in two, with Solomon's son, Rehoboam, ruling over only two of the twelve tribes. Wise King Solomon's reign had begun with great potential but ended in war, division, and failure.

DID YOU KNOW?

Solomon was proclaimed king even though he was not the oldest of David's sons.

STEPHEN | *THE FIRST CHRISTIAN MARTYR*

STORY IN BIBLE Acts 6–7

BORN First century AD

NAME MEANING "Crown"

OCCUPATION Deacon, food distributor

RELATIVES Unknown

CONTEMPORARIES Paul, the disciples

CLAIM TO FAME Died for his faith in Jesus

- One of seven deacons appointed by the disciples to distribute food to widows.
- Full of grace and the Holy Spirit
- Known for doing miracles and speaking boldly
- Arrested and condemned by the Sanhedrin
- Saw a vision of heaven opening and Jesus standing beside the Lord's throne
- Stoned to death with the approval of Saul (later Paul) for proclaiming Jesus as the Son of God
- Asked the Lord to forgive those who killed him

STORY IN BIBLE John 11; 20–21

INTRO First century AD

NAME MEANING Aramaic for "Twin"

OCCUPATION Apostle

RELATIVES Unknown

CONTEMPORARIES Jesus, the disciples

CLAIM TO FAME Doubted Jesus' resurrection

- Also called Didymus (Greek for "Twin")
- Willing to die with Jesus in Jerusalem
- Had a somewhat pessimistic personality
- Asked Jesus before His arrest to explain where He was going and how the disciples would go there with Him
- Did not believe Jesus had risen from the dead until Jesus appeared and showed Thomas His wounds
- Declared his faith that Jesus was truly God when he saw Jesus in person

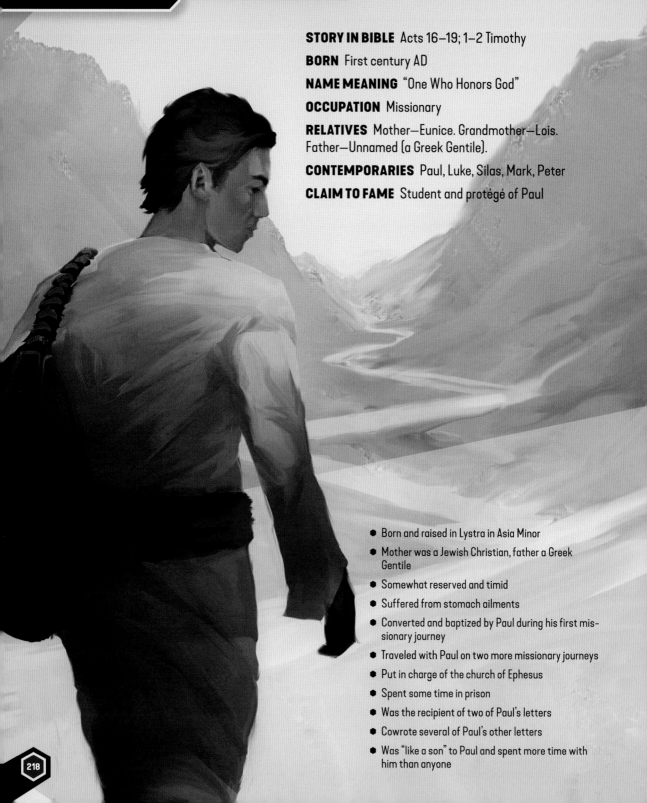

TIMOTHY
PAUL'S SPIRITUAL SON

STORY IN BIBLE Acts 16–19; 1–2 Timothy

BORN First century AD

NAME MEANING "One Who Honors God"

OCCUPATION Missionary

RELATIVES Mother—Eunice. Grandmother—Lois. Father—Unnamed (a Greek Gentile).

CONTEMPORARIES Paul, Luke, Silas, Mark, Peter

CLAIM TO FAME Student and protégé of Paul

- Born and raised in Lystra in Asia Minor
- Mother was a Jewish Christian, father a Greek Gentile
- Somewhat reserved and timid
- Suffered from stomach ailments
- Converted and baptized by Paul during his first missionary journey
- Traveled with Paul on two more missionary journeys
- Put in charge of the church of Ephesus
- Spent some time in prison
- Was the recipient of two of Paul's letters
- Cowrote several of Paul's other letters
- Was "like a son" to Paul and spent more time with him than anyone

STORY IN BIBLE 1–2 Corinthians; Galatians; 2 Timothy; Titus

BORN First century AD

NAME MEANING "Title of Honor" (uncertain)

OCCUPATION Missionary

RELATIVES Parents were Gentiles

CONTEMPORARIES Paul, Timothy

CLAIM TO FAME First Gentile accepted as a Christian by the church at Jerusalem

- Greek by birth
- Converted to Christianity by Paul
- First to be accepted as a Christian without having to conform to Jewish law
- Close friend and associate of Paul
- Skillful in resolving conflicts
- Sent by Paul to Corinth to repair the rift between Paul and the Corinthian church
- Collected a relief offering in Corinth to send to the Jerusalem church
- Put in charge of the struggling Christian church on the island of Crete, which was full of false teachers and conflict
- Encouraged in his ministry by a personal letter from Paul
- Called by Paul "my true child in the common faith"

UZZIAH | *A PLAGUED KING*

STORY IN BIBLE 2 Kings 14–15, 2 Chronicles 26

BORN Around 800 BC

NAME MEANING "The Lord Is My Strength"

OCCUPATION Tenth king of Judah

RELATIVES Father—King Amaziah. Mother—Jecoliah.

CONTEMPORARIES Isaiah, Hosea, Amos, Azariah the priest

CLAIM TO FAME Pride led to his downfall

- Crowned king at age sixteen after his father was assassinated.
- Called "Azariah" in 2 Kings
- Reigned for fifty-two years
- Did what was right in the eyes of the Lord
- Prospered in early years
- Famous for his military exploits and strong army
  - Became prideful in later years
    - Struck with leprosy by the Lord when he attempted to make an offering on the incense altar, something only priests were allowed to do
      - Forced to live in isolation the rest of his life and could not enter the temple
      - His son Jotham took over his duties until his death

STORY IN BIBLE Book of Esther, mentioned in Ezra

BORN 518 BC in Susa, capital of Persia

NAME MEANING "Ruling Over Heroes" (uncertain)

OCCUPATION King of Persia from 486 to 465 BC

RELATIVES Father—Darius the Great. Mother—Atossa (daughter of Cyrus the Great). First Wife—Vashti. Second Wife—Esther.

CLAIM TO FAME Almost wiped out the Jews of Persia

- Also known as Ahasuerus
- Ruler of Persian Empire, the world's superpower
- Held a feast that lasted 180 days
- Deposed his queen when she disobeyed his command to appear at the feast
- Chose Esther, a Jewish girl, as his next queen
- Was persuaded to sign an edict condemning all Jews in Persia to death
- Thanks to Esther, he wrote a second edict allowing the Jews to arm themselves and fight back
- Tried and failed to conquer Greece
- Murdered by his own bodyguard

ZACCHAEUS | A SINNER SAVED

STORY IN BIBLE Luke 19

BORN First century AD

NAME MEANING "Innocent"

OCCUPATION Chief tax collector of Jericho

RELATIVES Unknown

CONTEMPORARY Jesus

CLAIM TO FAME Climbed a tree to see Jesus

Zacchaeus had the most hated job in Judea: tax collector. Even the priests considered tax collectors beyond redemption because they took money from poor people and often cheated them.

But when Jesus came to Jericho, Zacchaeus wanted to see Him. The crowds were large, and he was short, so he ran ahead and climbed a sycamore tree to get a good view.

Jesus saw Zacchaeus in the tree and called to him by name. He told the tax collector to come down because Jesus was going to dine at his house that day. Zacchaeus was so overjoyed to meet Jesus that he decided to give half his possessions to the poor and to pay back four times over anyone he had cheated.

Although many people grumbled that Jesus had shown compassion to such a sinful man, Jesus declared that He had come to "seek and to save the lost." That day, a lost soul was found again.

ZECHARIAH

STORY IN BIBLE Luke 1

BORN Around 50 BC

NAME MEANING "The Lord Remembered"

OCCUPATION Priest

RELATIVES Wife—Elizabeth. Son—John the Baptist.

CONTEMPORARIES Mary, Jesus

CLAIM TO FAME Told by an angel he would have a son

- Priest in the line of Aaron
- In Abijah's division (there were twenty-four priestly divisions, each assigned to serve in the temple for two weeks each year)
- Obedient and blameless in God's eyes
- Older in years and childless
- Selected by lot to burn incense in the Holy Place—a job given only once in a lifetime

An angel appeared to Zechariah the day he went into the temple to burn incense. The angel told him that Zechariah's wife, Elizabeth, would have a child, and he was to name the child John. John would be a great man, the angel said, and would prepare the people for the coming of the Lord.

Zechariah was terrified of the angel at first. But then he was doubtful. Elizabeth was long past the age of child-bearing, he replied. Besides, she was barren.

Zechariah's words angered the angel, who said, "I am Gabriel, who stands in the presence of God." And because of Zechariah's doubt, Gabriel told him he would not speak again until the child was born.

Sure enough, Elizabeth had a son several months later. Relatives and friends gathered to celebrate the miraculous birth, and while everyone told Zechariah to name the boy after himself, the old priest demanded a writing tablet and wrote: "His name is John."

And then Zechariah got his voice back.

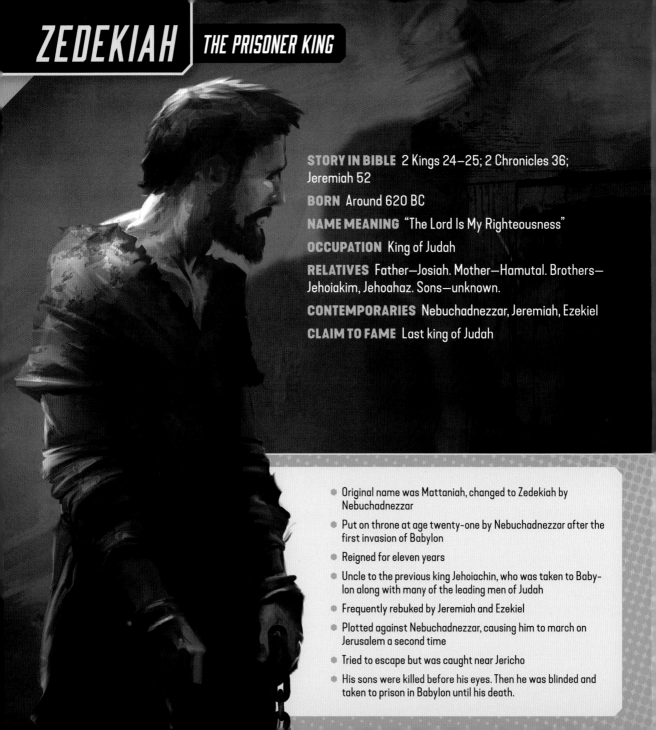

ZEDEKIAH | *THE PRISONER KING*

STORY IN BIBLE 2 Kings 24–25; 2 Chronicles 36; Jeremiah 52

BORN Around 620 BC

NAME MEANING "The Lord Is My Righteousness"

OCCUPATION King of Judah

RELATIVES Father—Josiah. Mother—Hamutal. Brothers—Jehoiakim, Jehoahaz. Sons—unknown.

CONTEMPORARIES Nebuchadnezzar, Jeremiah, Ezekiel

CLAIM TO FAME Last king of Judah

- Original name was Mattaniah, changed to Zedekiah by Nebuchadnezzar
- Put on throne at age twenty-one by Nebuchadnezzar after the first invasion of Babylon
- Reigned for eleven years
- Uncle to the previous king Jehoiachin, who was taken to Babylon along with many of the leading men of Judah
- Frequently rebuked by Jeremiah and Ezekiel
- Plotted against Nebuchadnezzar, causing him to march on Jerusalem a second time
- Tried to escape but was caught near Jericho
- His sons were killed before his eyes. Then he was blinded and taken to prison in Babylon until his death.